Liberty Hyde Bailey

Plant-Breeding

Five Lectures Upon the Amelioration of Domestic Plants

Liberty Hyde Bailey

Plant-Breeding

Five Lectures Upon the Amelioration of Domestic Plants

ISBN/EAN: 9783337143992

Printed in Europe, USA, Canada, Australia, Japan

Cover: Foto ©Andreas Hilbeck / pixelio.de

More available books at **www.hansebooks.com**

PLANT-BREEDING

BEING FIVE LECTURES UPON THE AMELIORATION OF DOMESTIC PLANTS

BY

L. H. BAILEY

New York
THE MACMILLAN COMPANY
LONDON: MACMILLAN & CO., Ltd.
1897

All rights reserved

COPYRIGHT, 1895,
BY L. H. BAILEY.

Set up and electrotyped December, 1895. Reprinted
April, 1896; August, 1897.

Norwood Press
J. S. Cushing & Co. — Berwick & Smith
Norwood Mass. U.S.A.

PREFACE.

There is no subject associated with the care of plants respecting which there is so much misapprehension and imperfect knowledge, as that of the origination of new forms. Most of the scattered writing touching it treats the subject as if all our knowledge of the matter were and must be derived wholly from experiment. It therefore recites examples of how this and that new form has come to be, and has made little attempt to discover the fundamental causes of the genesis of the novelties. Horticulturists commonly look upon each novelty as an isolated fact, whilst we ought to regard each one as but an expression of some law of the variation of plants. It is the common notion, too, to consider any type of plant to be essentially a fixed entity, and to regard any marked departure from the type as a phenomenon rather more to be wondered at than to be explained. It is evident, however, that one cannot understand the production of new varieties until he has grasped some of the fundamental principles of the onward progression of the vegetable kingdom. Any attempt, therefore, to explain the origin of garden varieties, and the methods of producing them, must be at the same time a contribution to the literature of the philosophy of organic evolution.

I do not know of any explicit and sustained attempt to account for the evolution of all garden forms, and I have therefore brought together in this volume the subject-matter of various lectures which I have been in the habit of giving before my students. The first and third lectures were newly elaborated the present summer for two addresses before the class in biology which came together at the University of Pennsylvania, under the auspices of the American Society for the Extension of University Teaching. The second lecture was first presented before the Massachusetts State Board of Agriculture, in Boston, December 1, 1891. In April, 1892, it was republished, with a bibliography of the subject, by the Rural Publishing Co., under the title, "Cross-Breeding and Hybridizing." This publication is now out of print. I have made no attempt to collect lists or catalogues of varieties, but have endeavored to make very brief statements of some of the underlying principles of the amelioration of plants, with only sufficient examples to fix them in the mind.

I hope that teachers of horticulture and botany may find the book useful in their classes. When it is necessary to abridge the instruction or to present it to untrained students, only Lectures III. and V. may be used, for these contain the matters of greatest demonstrative importance.

L. H. BAILEY.

CORNELL UNIVERSITY,
ITHACA, N.Y., September 1, 1895.

CONTENTS.

LECTURE I.

	PAGE
THE FACT AND PHILOSOPHY OF VARIATION	1
I. *The Fact of Individuality*	2
The seed-individual.	
The bud-individual.	
II. *The Causes of Individual Differences*	8
a. Fortuitous variation	9
b. Sex as a factor in the variation of plants	11
c. Physical environment and variation	12
1. Variation in food supply	16
2. Variation in climate	24
3. Change of seed. Bud-variation	28
d. Struggle for life a cause of variation	29
III. *The Choice and Fixation of Variations*	31

LECTURE II.

THE PHILOSOPHY OF THE CROSSING OF PLANTS, CONSIDERED IN REFERENCE TO THEIR IMPROVEMENT UNDER CULTIVATION	39
I. *The Struggle for Life*	39
II. *The Division of Labor*	42
III. *The Limits of Crossing*	44

CONTENTS.

	PAGE
IV. *Function of the Cross*	50
a. The gradual amelioration of the type	50
b. Change of seed and crossing	59
c. The outright production of new varieties	64
V. *Characteristics of Crosses*	68
VI. *Uncertainties of Pollination*	83
Conclusion	86

LECTURE III.

How Domestic Varieties Originate 87

I. *Indeterminate Varieties* 87

II. *Plant-breeding* 91

   Rule 1. Antagonistic features . . . 95
   Rule 2. Quickest results in the most variable groups 96
   Rule 3. Breed for one thing at a time . . 98
   Rule 4. Contradictory attributes . . . 98
   Rule 5. Characters of the entire plant most important 99
   Rule 6. Plants differ in hereditary power . 104
   Rule 7. Less marked variations more important 105
   Rule 8. Crossing a means, not an end . . 107
   Rule 9. Choice of parents to a cross . . 109
   Rule 10. The ideal should be mental . . 112
   Rule 11. Seek to produce variation in the desired direction 114
   Rule 12. Watch for bud-varieties . . . 118
   Rule 13. Progress lies in selection . . . 120
   Rule 14. The type is kept up to standard by continued selection . . . 122
   Rule 15. The best final results are to be obtained by high tillage and intelligent selection 127

CONTENTS. xi

	PAGE
III. *Specific Examples*	129
The dewberry and blackberry . . .	129
The apple	131
Beans	135
Cannas	140

LECTURE IV.

BORROWED OPINIONS; BEING EXTRACTS FROM THE WRITINGS OF B. VERLOT, E. A. CARRIÈRE, AND W. O. FOCKE 143

I. *Verlot's Classification of Varieties of Ornamental Plants* 143

II. *Carrière's Account of Bud-varieties* . . 153
    1. General remarks upon bud-variation . . 154
    2. List of bud-varieties 176

III. *Focke's Discussion of the Characteristics of Crosses* 215
    i. The simple primary cross 215
        Proposition 1. Similarity of crossed offspring 215
        Proposition 2. Dissimilarity of crossed offspring 221
        Proposition 3. Vegetative powers of hybrids 225
        Proposition 4. Comparative fertility of hybrids 228
        Proposition 5. Malformations in hybrid offspring 237
    ii. The progeny of crosses 237
        1. Progeny of crosses with their own pollen 238

CONTENTS.

	PAGE
2. Derivative hybridization of crosses with the parent forms	242
3. Hybrids of several species	244
a. Triple hybrids	244
b. Hybrids of four to six species	246
c. Crosses of plants grown together	247
iii. Cross-breeds and hybrids	247

LECTURE V.

POLLINATION; OR HOW TO CROSS PLANTS . . . 252

    I. *The Structure of the Flower* 252

    II. *Manipulating the Flowers* 265

GLOSSARY 282

INDEX 286

PLANT-BREEDING.

LECTURE I.

THE FACT AND PHILOSOPHY OF VARIATION.

THERE is no one fact connected with horticulture which so greatly interests all persons as the existence of numerous varieties of plants which seem to satisfy every need of the gardener. Whence came all this multitude of forms? What are the methods employed in securing them? Are they simply isolated facts or phenomena of gardening, or have they some relation to the broader phases of the evolution of the forms of life? These are some of the questions which occur to every reflective mind when it contemplates an attractive garden, but they are questions which seem never to be answered. Whatever attempt the gardener may make at answering them is either befogged by an effort to define what a variety is, or else it consists in simply reciting how a few given varieties came to be known. But there must be some fundamental method of arriving at a conception of how the varieties of fruits and flowers and other cultivated plants have originated. If there is no such method, then the origination of these varieties must follow no law, and the discussion of the whole subject is fruitless. But we have every confidence in the consecutive uniformity of the operations of nature, and it were strange if some underlying principle of the unfolding or progression of plant life does not dominate the origin of the varied and innumerable varieties which, from time unknown, have responded to the touch of the cultivator. Let us first, therefore, make a broad survey of the subject in a philosophical spirit, and, later, discuss the more specific instances of the origination of varieties.

I. The Fact of Individuality.

There is universal difference in nature. No two living things are exact counterparts, for no two are born into exactly the same conditions and experiences. Every living object has individuality; that is, there is something about it which enables the acute observer to distinguish it from all other objects, even of the same class or species. Every plant in a row of lettuce is different from every other plant, and the gardener, when transplanting them, selects out, almost unconsciously, some plants which please him and others which do not. Every apple tree in an orchard of a thousand Baldwins is unlike every other one, perhaps in size or shape, or possibly in the vigor of growth or the kind of fruit it bears. Persons who buy apples for export know that fruit from certain regions stands the shipments better than the same variety from other regions; and if one were to go into the orchards where these apples are grown, he would find the owner still further refining the problem by talking about the merits of individual trees in his orchard. If one were to make the effort, he would find that it is possible to distinguish differences between every two spears of grass in a meadow, or every two heads of wheat in a grain-field.

All this is equivalent to saying that plants are infinitely variable. The ultimate causes of all this variation are beyond the purpose of the present discussion, but it must be evident, to the reflective mind, that these differences are the means of adapting the innumerable individuals to every little difference or advantage in the environment in which they live. And if the object of variation is better adaptation to the physical conditions of life, then the same motive must have been present in the circumstances which determined the birth of the individual. The variation in environment, therefore, must be the cause of much of the variation in plants, since differences in plants were positively injurious if it were possible for the conditions of environment to be the same.

If no two plants are anywhere alike, then it is not strange if now and then some departure, more marked than common, is named and becomes a garden variety. We have been taught to feel that plants are essentially stable and inelastic, and that any departure from the type is an exception and calls for immediate explanation. The fact is, however, that plants are essentially unstable and plastic, and that variation between the individuals must everywhere be expected. This erroneous notion of the stability of organisms comes of our habit of studying what we call species. We set for ourselves a type of plant or animal, and group about it all those individuals which are more like this type than they are like any other, and this group we name a species. Nowadays, the species is regarded as nothing more than a convenient and arbitrary expression for classifying our knowledge of the forms of life, but the older naturalists conceived that the species is the real entity or unit in nature, and we have not yet wholly outgrown the habit of mind which was born of that fallacy. Nature knows nothing about species; she is concerned with the individual, the ultimate unit. This individual she moulds and fits into the chinks of environment, and each individual tends to become the more unlike its birthmates the more the environments of the various individuals are unlike. I would impress upon you, therefore, as a fundamental conception to the discussion of the general subject before us, the importance of the individual plant, rather than the importance of the species; for thereby we put ourselves as nearly as possible in a sympathetic attitude with nature, and, resting upon the ultimate object of her concern, we are able to understand what may be conceived to be her motive in working out the problem of life. That I may still more forcibly emphasize this thought, let me recall to your minds the fact that the whole tendency of contemporary civilization, in sociology and religion, is to deal with the individual person and not with the mass. This is only an unconscious feeling after natural methods of solving the most complex of problems, for it is exactly the means to which every organic thing has been subjected from the beginning.

In looking for the ultimate unit or individuality or personality in nature, we must make a broad distinction between the animal and the plant. Every higher animal is itself a unit; it is one. It has a more or less definite span of life, and every part and organ contribute a certain indispensable part to the life and personality of the organism. No part is capable of propagating itself independently of the sex-organs of the animal, nor is it capable of developing sex-organs of its own. If any part is removed, the animal is maimed and perhaps it dies. The plant, on the contrary, has no definite or distinct autonomy. Most plants live an indefinite existence, dependent very closely upon the immediate conditions in which they grow. Every part or branch of the plant lives largely for itself, it is capable of propagating and multiplying itself when removed from the parent plant or the colony of branches of which it is a member, and it develops sex-organs and other individual features of its own. If any branch is removed, the tree or plant does not necessarily suffer; in fact, the remaining branches usually profit by the removal, a fact which shows that there is a competition, or struggle for existence, between the different branches or elements of the plant. The whole theory and practice of pruning rest upon the fact of the individual unlikenesses of the branches of plants; and these unlikenesses are of the same kind and often of the same degree as those which exist between different plants which are grown from seeds. That is, the branches of a Crawford peach tree, for example, differ amongst themselves in size, shape, vigor, productiveness, and season of maturity, the same as any two or more separate Crawford trees, or any number of trees of other varieties, differ the one from the others. If any one of these branches or buds is removed and is grown into an independent tree, a person could not tell — if he were ignorant of its history — if this tree were derived from a branch or a seed. This proves that there is no essential unlikeness between branches and independent plants, except the mere accident that one grows upon another branch or plant whilst the other grows in the ground. But the branch may be severed and grown in the ground, and the seedling may be pulled up and grafted on the tree, and no one can distinguish the different origins of the two. And then, as a matter of fact, a very large proportion of our cultivated plants are not distinct plants at all, in the sense of being different creations from seeds, but are simply the results of the division of branches of one original plant or branch. All the fruit trees of any one variety are obtained from the dividing up and multiplication of the branches of the first or original tree.

You are now curious to know how this original tree came to be, and this I hope to tell you before I am done; but for the present, let me impress it upon you that it is equally possible for it to have come from a seed, or to have sprung from a branch which some person had noticed to be very different from the associated branches in the tree-top. In other words, the ultimate unit or individual in growing plants is the bud and the bit of wood or tissue to which it is attached; for every bud, like every seed, produces an offspring which can be distinguished from every other offspring whatsoever.

II. The Causes of Individual Differences.

We have now gotten back to the starting-point, to that unit with which nature begins to make her initial differences or individualities; that is, to the point where variations arise. This unit is the bud and the seed, — one sexless, or the offspring of one parent; the other sexual, or the offspring of two parents. Now, inasmuch as the horticultural variety is only a well-marked variation which the gardener has chanced to notice and to propagate, it follows that the only logical method of determining how garden varieties originate is to discover the means by which plants vary or differ one from another.

There is probably no one fact of organic nature concerning the origin of which modern philosophers are so much divided as the genesis or reasons for the beginnings of variations or differences. It seems to be an inscrutable problem, and it would be useless, therefore, for us to attempt to discover these ultimate forces in the present hour. Still, we must give them sufficient thought to enable us to satisfy our minds as to how far these variations may be produced by man; and, in doing this, we must discover at least the underlying philosophy of plant variation. It is the nature of organisms to be unlike their parents and their birthmates. Why?

a. *Fortuitous Variation.*

It will probably never be possible to refer every variation to a distinct cause, for it is probable that some of them have no antecedent. If we conceive of the forms of life as having been created with characters exactly uniform from generation to generation, then we should be led to look for a distinct occasion or cause for every departure from the type; but we know, as I have already pointed out, that heredity by its very nature is not so exact as to carry over every attribute, and no other, of the parent to the offspring. Elasticity, plasticity, is a part of the essential constitution of all organic beings. There is probably no inherent tendency in organisms towards any ultimate or predetermined completion of form, as the older naturalists supposed, but simply a laxity or indefiniteness of constitution which is expressed in numberless minor differences in individuals.

That is, some variation is simply fortuitous, an inevitable result of the inherent plasticity of organisms, and it has no immediate inciting cause. If we were to assume that every minor difference is the result of some immediate cause, then we should expect every individual plant or animal to fill some niche, to satisfy some need, to produce the definite effect for which the cause stands. But it is apparent to one who contemplates the operations of nature that very many — certainly more than half — of the organisms which are born are wholly useless in the struggle for life and very soon perish. From these fortuitous variations nature selects, to be sure, many individuals to be the parents of other generations because they chance to be fitted to live, but this does not affect the methods or reasons of their origin. It is possible that, whilst many of these mere individual differences have no direct and immediate cause, they may still be the result of a devious line of antecedent causes long since so much diffused and modified that they will remain forever unrecognizable; but even if so, the fact still remains that these present differences or variations may be purposeless, and it is quite as well to say that they exist because it is a part of the organic constitution of living things that unlike produces unlike.

b. *Sex as a Factor in the Variation of Plants.*

All plants have the faculty, either potential or expressed, of propagating themselves by means of buds, or asexual parts. This is obviously the cheapest and most direct possible method of propagation for many-membered plants, since it requires no special reproductive organization and energy, and, as only one parent is concerned in it, there is none of the risk of failure which resides in any mode of propagation in which two parents must find each other and form a union. There must be some reason, therefore, for the existence of such a costly mechanism as sex aside from its use as a mere means of propagation. It may be said that it exists because it is a means of more rapid multiplication than bud-propagation, but such is not necessarily the fact. There are many plants which produce buds as freely as they produce seeds; and then, if mere multiplication were the only destiny of the plant, bud-production would no doubt have greatly increased to have met the demand for new generations. The only reason for the existence of sex in the vegetable world seems to be the need for a constant rejuvenation and modification of the offspring by uniting the features of two individuals into one. There thus arises from every sexual union a number of new or different forms from which nature may select the best, — that is, those best fitted to live in the conditions in which they chance to be placed. But whilst sex is undoubtedly one of the most potent sources of present unlikenesses, it is not necessarily an original cause of individual differences, since the two parties to any sexual contract must be unlike before they can produce unlike. When once the initial unlikenesses were established, every new sexual union would produce new combinations, so that now, when every new form, from whatever source it appears, comes into existence, there are other intimately related forms with which it may cross. This state of things has existed to a greater or less degree from the moment sex first appeared, so that the organic world is now endlessly varied as the result of a most complex ancestry.

The variety which sexual union has introduced into the world performs such an important part in the evolution of the forms of plants, and the problems which it presents are so complex, that I shall leave the whole subject for an independent discussion (Lecture II.).

c. *Physical Environment and Variation.*

Every phase and condition of physical circumstances, which are not absolutely prohibitive of plant life, have plants which thrive in them.

ENVIRONMENT AND VARIATION.

Every soil and climate, every degree of humidity, hills, swamps, and ponds,— every place is filled with plants. Even the trunks and branches of trees support other plants, as epiphytes and parasites. That is, plants have adapted themselves to every physical environment; or, to turn the proposition around, every physical environment produces adaptive changes in plants. There are those, like Weismann and his adherents, who contend, from purely speculative reasons, that these changes do not become hereditary or permanent until they have influenced a certain physiological substance which is assumed to reside in the reproductive regions of the organism, and that all those changes which have not yet reached this germ-plasm are, therefore, lost, or die with the organism. It is not necessary to combat this philosophy, for we know, as a matter of common horticultural experience, that every change or variation in any organism — unless it proceeds from mere accident or mutilation — may become hereditary or be the beginning of a new variety; it is only necessary, therefore, for the Weismannians to assume — as they are always ready to do — that any variation which has become fixed or permanent has already affected the germ. Their assumption needs only another assumption to prove it, and, therefore, when we are considering merely plain matters of fact and experience, we need give little attention to the subtleties of this Neo-Darwinian philosophy.

Weismann teaches that "acquired characters," or those variations which first appear in the lifetime of the individual because of the influences of environment, are lost, because they have not yet affected the reproductive substance. But if these characters are induced by the effect of impinging environment during two or more generations, they may come to be so persistent that the plant cannot throw them off, and they become, thereby, a part of the hereditary and non-negotiable property of the species. Now, it is apparent that in one or another of the generations which are thus acted upon by the environment, there must be a beginning towards the fixing or hereditable permanency of the new form, and we might as well assume that this beginning takes place in the first generation as in the last, since there can be no proof that it does not take place in either one. The tendency towards fixity, if it exists at all, undoubtedly originates at the very time that the variation itself originates, and it is only sophistry to assume that the form appears at one time and the tendency towards permanence at another time. Since plants fit themselves into their circumstances by means of adaptive variations, we must conclude that all adaptive variations have the power of persisting, upon occasion.

All these remarks, whilst somewhat abstruse, have a most important bearing upon the philosophy of the origin of garden varieties, because they show, first, that changes in the conditions in which plants grow introduce modifications in the plants themselves, and second, that wherever any modification occurs it is probable that it may be fixed and perpetuated.

It is necessary, at this point, that we distinguish between natal and post-natal variations; that is, between those variations which are born with plants, and those which appear, as a result of environment, after the plant has begun to grow. It is commonly assumed that the form and general characters of the plant are already determined in the seed, but a moment's reflection will show that this is far from the truth. One may sow a hundred selected peas, for instance, all of which may be alike in every discernible character. If these are planted in a space a foot square, it will be found, after two or three weeks, that some individuals are outstripping the others, although all of them came up equally well and were at first practically indistinguishable. This means that, because of a little advantage in food or moisture, or other circumstance, some plants have obtained the mastery and are crowding out the less fortunate ones. Here is a variation taking place before our very eyes, and we may be able to see the exact cause of it. Moreover, variations which originate in this way may pass down to the offspring through the seeds, as in the case of "viney" peas, which are grown on too rich soil. All this is a matter of the commonest observation with the gardener, who is so accustomed to seeing great differences arise in batches of plants, all of which start equal and with an equal chance, that he never thinks to comment upon the occurrence. In fact, the theory and practice of agriculture rest upon the fact that plants can be modified greatly by the conditions in which they grow, after they have become thoroughly established in the soil. Plants may start equal, but may differ widely at the harvest; and this difference may be controlled to a nicety by the cultivator. Every farmer knows, too, that the best results for the succeeding year are to be got only when he selects seeds from the best which he has been able to produce this year. So, given uniformity or equality at the start, the operator moulds the individual plants largely at his will.

Having noticed that physical environments may modify plants, we are now ready to consider just what changes in these circumstances of plant life are most fruitful in the production of new forms.

1. *Variation in Food Supply.* — The greater part of the changes in the physical conditions of life hinge upon the relative supply of food.

Climbing plants assume their form because, by virtue of the divergence of character, they are enabled to fit themselves into places which other plants cannot occupy. They rear their foliage into the air, where food and sunlight are unappropriated. The lower branches of the tree-top die, and the others thereby appropriate the more food and grow the faster. The entire practice of agriculture is built upon the augmentation of the food supply. For this purpose, we set the plants in isolated positions, we till the ground, keep down other plants or weeds, add plant food to the soil, and prune the tree and thin the fruit.

Thomas Andrew Knight, the chief of horticultural philosophers, appears to have been the first to clearly enunciate the law that excess of food supply is the most prolific cause of the variation of plants. Darwin subscribes to it without reserve: "Of all the causes which induce variability, excess of food, whether or not changed in nature, is probably the most powerful." Alexander Braun, an earlier writer upon the philosophy of the organic world, said that "it appears rather, on the whole, as if the unusual conditions favorable to a luxuriant state of development, afforded by cultivation, awakened in the plant the inward impulse to the display of all those variations possible within the more or less narrowly circumscribed limits of the species." It is generally agreed by those who have given the matter much thought, that an excess of food above the amount normally or habitually received is one of the very chief, if not the most dominant, causes of individual differences in plants. Certainly every farmer and gardener knows that the richer the soil in available plant food, the stronger and the more abnormal and unusual his product will be.

If, then, excess of food supply is a strong factor in the modification of plants, and if the one fundamental aim of agriculture is to supply food in excess of natural conditions, it must naturally follow that cultivated plants should be of all others the most variable. This is notably true. Now, the first variation which usually comes of this liberal food supply is increase in mere bigness. Probably every plant which has ever been cultivated has increased its stature or the size of some or all of its parts. Moreover, this is generally the direct object of cultivation, — to secure larger herbage, fruits, seeds, or flowers. Incidentally, we find here an indubitable proof of the truth of the hypothesis of evolution, for if it were impossible for plants to vary or to assume new characters, there would be no cultivation and no agriculture; for there would be little object in cultivating a product if it grew equally well in the wild.

This variation into mere bigness is more important than it may seem at first sight. All thoughtful horticulturists agree in believing that the first thing to be done in ameliorating any plant is to "break the type," that is, to cause it to vary. The particular direction of variation is not so important, at first; for all experience has shown that if once the seedlings of a plant begin to depart from the parental type, other and various modifications will soon follow. If a plant is once strongly modified in size, variations in shape, color, flavor, or other attributes are forthcoming. This apparent accumulation of variation seems at first to be incapable of scientific explanation, but the reasons for it are not difficult to understand when once they are presented.

When plants are placed in new conditions, whether in the wild or in cultivation, then they begin to vary, but usually only in one direction at first, although the amount of the variation, and sometimes the kind, is determined very largely by the nature and the extent of the change in the conditions. This initial variation, particularly when plants are transferred to cultivated areas, is generally in the direction of greater size consequent upon the greater amount of food. This initial variation is generally soon followed by others in various directions, and from these the cultivator may be able to establish new varieties. We now ask ourselves why these many variations appear when once the type begins to modify itself. Consider the fact that the world is now full of plants. In untamed nature, not one more plant can grow unless another plant dies. All plants, therefore, are held down to narrow limits of numbers, and since there are so few individuals, — in comparison with the seeds and buds which each plant produces for the chance of multiplying itself, — there must be, also, few kinds and degrees of individual differences. The farther and more freely a plant distributes itself, the greater must be the differences between the various individuals, because they must adapt themselves to a wider range of conditions. All plants are held in equilibrium, so to speak; but the plant organism is plastic by nature and quickly responds to every touch of environment; so, as soon as the pressure is removed in any direction, the plant at once springs into the breach. Recall the monotonous vegetation of the deep forest, where the battle of centuries has subdued all but the strongest. Clear away the forest, and then observe the fierce scramble for place and life amongst a multitude of forms which spring in for an opportunity to better their conditions. In a few years more, the tender low herbs have gone. The briars and underbrush have usurped the land. As time goes on, one species after another perishes, and when the place is again reforested, two or three species hold undisputed sway over the land. The poplars which followed the pines have long since perished and pines again dominate the forest. Or, if the area were turned to pasture a few years after the woods were removed, the herbs and bushes die with the browsing, and in time the June grass covers the whole landscape with the mantle of conquest. So plants may be said to be always ready to fill new places in the polity of nature by adapting themselves to the new circumstances as they grow into them. The appearing of any one marked variation, therefore, is evidence that the plant has found a new condition, that the pressure is somewhat lifted, and that its whole plastic organization will soon respond to the new environment. It is apparent, then, how the simplest and rudest cultivation has been able, through the centuries, to so profoundly modify our domestic plants that we are often unable to recognize the forms from which they sprung.

We must not forget to notice, at this point, that the food supply differs amongst the various branches of the same plant. Some branches, by reason of position with reference to the main trunk or with reference to air and sunlight, or, because of a better start in the beginning as a result of some incidental advantage, gain the mastery over others and crowd them out. We have already seen that no two branches on a plant are alike; and we are now able to understand that sports or bud-varieties are no more inexplicable than seed-varieties are.

Cultivation is really but an extension or intensification of nature's methods of dealing with the plant world. The ultimate object of both nature and man is to supply more food. The variations which arise from the effects of mere cultivation, therefore, are in kind very like those which nature produces, the chief difference being that of degree. The accustomed operations of the farmer, therefore, have been powerful agents in the evolution of vegetable forms. The ways in which cultivation affords a more liberal food supply are as follows:—

1. By isolating the individual plant. The husbandman sets each plant by itself, and then protects it by destroying the weeds or plants which endeavor to crowd it out. There is a partial exception to this in the "sowed crops," like the grains, and it is noticeable that variation in these plants is usually less marked than in the "hoed crops."

2. By giving the plant the advantage of position, whereby it is allowed the most congenial exposure to sun and contour of land.

3. By increasing the fertility of the soil, either by tillage or the direct application of plant

food, or both. Rich and moist soils tend to "break" the type,—or to cause initial variations,—to produce verdant colors and loss of saccharine and pungent qualities, to induce redundant growth, and to delay maturity and thereby to render plants tender to cold winter climates.

4. By thinning the tops of plants and the fruits, whereby the remaining parts receive an amount of food in excess of the habitual allowance.

5. By divergence of character in associated plants. It is well known that a field which is planted so thickly to corn that it cannot grow more with profit, may still grow pumpkins between. The pumpkins and the corn are so unlike in form that they complement each other, the one filling the niche which the other is not fitted to occupy. We have already seen that a copse ever so full of bushes may still grow vines. A meadow which is full of timothy may still grow clover in the bottom, and land which is covered with apple trees still grows weeds beneath. "The more diversified the descendants from any one species become in structure, constitution, and habits," writes Darwin, "by so much will they be better enabled to seize on many and widely diversified places in the polity of nature, and so be enabled to increase in numbers."

2. *Variation in Climate.* — The fact that any distinct climatic region usually has plants which are very closely related to those of other climatic regions in the same zone, points strongly to the probable profound modification of plants by climate. And, furthermore, we should expect that if the food environment modifies plants, the climatic environment must have the same power. Moreover, there is abundant historical and experimental proof that climate is capable of greatly modifying the vegetable kingdom. There are those who contradict any great effect of climate in the variation of plants, and acclimatization has been even stoutly denied. These persons make the mistake of asking that a visible modification take place at once upon the transfer of a plant from one climate to another, and they also err in supposing that a plant can adapt itself to a cold climate only by developing a capability to withstand more cold. Indian corn is sometimes cited as proof that plants do not become acclimatized, for it is as tender to frost now as ever, for all that we know. Yet this very plant affords a most unequivocal example of complete acclimatization, because it has shortened its period of growth fully one-half to enable it to escape the cold of the north.

The influence of a change of climate upon plants, or, what may amount to the same thing, the result of a transfer of plants to new climates, is so complex and so general that no detailed discussion of the subject can be made at this time. It will answer our present purpose to briefly designate the ways in which climate modifies plants: —

1. Climate greatly modifies the stature of plants. They become dwarfer in high latitudes and altitudes.

2. It modifies form. Plants tend to be broader-headed, and also more prostrate, in high latitudes and altitudes.

3. Proportionate leafiness generally increases, at the same time.

4. There is, also, often a gain in comparative fruitfulness following transfer towards the poles.

5. The colors of leaves, flowers, fruits, and seeds are greatly influenced by climate, there being a general tendency, in plants of temperate regions, to augmentation in intensity of colors as they are carried towards the poles.

6. There is modification in the flavor and essential ingredients of various parts, following a change of climate.

7. There is a variation in variability itself. The more difficult the climate in which a plant finds itself, the more it tends to vary to meet the uncongenial environments. In the high north, many plants are so variable that the marks used to identify the species in other latitudes are often lost.

8. There may be a profound variation or modification in constitution and habit by which plants become acclimatized, or enabled to endure a climate at first injurious to them. This may occur by a variation in the constitution of the descendants, which enables them to endure directly more untoward conditions. It generally comes about, however, through a change in habit, by which plants, when transferred towards the poles, shorten their season of growth or even become annuals. Plants become more sensitive to spring temperatures in cold climates, so that they start relatively much earlier in the season — that is, at a lower sum-temperature — than they do in warm climates. Any one who has passed the springtime in both the North and South must have noticed how much more suddenly the vegetation comes forward in the North; and it is surprising how the spring-sowed crops accelerate their growth in the North over those in the South.

The characters which result from a change of climatic environment are peculiarly within the control of the agriculturist, for a leading factor in his business is the transfer of plants far and wide over the earth. So it has come that the staple varieties of the important grains and fruits are unlike in Europe and America and in all great geographical areas, although all the various forms may have sprung from one ancestor within historic times. A new country is stocked with varieties from the mother country; but in the course of a few generations it is found that the varieties in cultivation are unlike the ones originally introduced, and from which they came. As wild plants have become separated from each other as species in the different geographical regions, so the cultivated plants soon begin to follow similar lines of divergence. In the beginning of the colonization of this country, for example, all the varieties of apples were of European origin. But in 1817, over sixty per cent of the apples recommended for cultivation here were of American origin, that is, American-grown seedlings from the original stock. At the present time, fully ninety per cent of the popular apples of the Atlantic states are American productions. The northern states of the Mississippi valley, to which most of our eastern apples are not adapted, are now witnessing a similar transformation in the adaptation and modification of the varieties introduced from the East and from Russia. The newly introduced Japanese plums are conceded to be great acquisitions to our fruit-growing, but no doubt the best results are yet to come with the origination of domestic varieties of them. So there is an irresistible tendency towards a divergence of forms in different continental or geographical regions, and much of the inevitable result is no doubt chargeable to climatic environment.

3. *Change of seed. Bud-variation.* — I will pause for a moment to consider two agencies or phenomena which are often associated with the genesis of varieties. One of these is the fact that the simple change of seed from one locality to another generally gives a larger or better product or even more marked variation. Mere transfer of seed is not of itself, however, a cause of variation. The change is beneficial because it fits together characters and environments which are not in equilibrium with each other. A plant which is grown for several years in one set of conditions becomes fitted into them, so to speak, and is in a comparative state of rest. When the plant or its progeny is taken to other conditions, all the adjustments are broken up, and in the refitting to the new circumstances new or strange characters are apt to appear. We shall leave this subject for the present, expecting to give it a fuller treatment in the second lecture.

Bud-variation, or sport, is a name given to those branches which are so much unlike the normal plant in any particular that they attract attention. Many garden varieties are simply multiplications of such abnormal branches. This bud-variation is commonly held to be such an unusual and inexplicable phenomenon that it is considered apart from all the general discussions of variation. It is not, of course, a cause of variability, but simply an effect of some antecedent, the same as seed-variation is. We have already seen that all the different branches, or even joints, of any plant are, in a very important sense, distinct individuals, since every one develops its own organs, each is capable of reproducing itself independently, and each is unlike every other because it is acted upon differently by environment and food supply. It is not strange, therefore, that some of these individuals should now and then depart very widely from the ordinary type, and thereby attract the attention of a gardener, who would forthwith make cuttings or set grafts from the part. Every branch is a bud-variety, just as truly as every seedling is a seed-variety, — since no seedling is ever exactly like its parent, — and there should be no greater mystery connected with the sports of buds than there is with the variations from seeds, for the causes which produce the one may be and are equally competent to produce the other.

d. *Struggle for Life a Cause of Variation.*

We have seen that the world is full of plants. There is room for more only as the present individuals die. Yet nearly every species produces a great number of seeds, and makes a most strenuous effort to multiply its kind. Any one plant, if left to itself, is capable of covering the earth in a comparatively short time. A fierce struggle for a chance to live is therefore inevitable. This conflict is most apparent to the general observer in the springtime, when every "herb yielding seed after his kind, and the tree yielding fruit, whose seed was in itself, after his kind," are sending forth a host of sturdy offspring. The very land seems to be pregnant with weeds and aspiring young growths. But by midsummer the numbers may be less. The weaker and less fortunate ones have perished, and the victors have waxed stronger thereby. The annual and half of the biennial species complete their course upon the approach of winter, and the older perennial herbs are becoming weak; so in the succeeding springtime there is again a fierce combat for the vacant places.

One of the results of this conflict is the adjustment of plants to each other. We have seen how the climbing plant insinuates itself in amongst the shrubberies and ties them together in an impenetrable tangle in order that it, itself, may have a chance to live. So the low plants of the deep forest are such as have been plastic enough to adapt themselves to the damp shades. Thus plants have developed companionships or divergences in characters, by means of which, under the stress of circumstances, they are able to live together. Plants have adapted themselves to other plants as truly as they have adapted themselves to soil or climate; and if these latter environments are ever the sources or causes of variation, then the first must be also. I must look upon the struggle for existence, therefore, as itself a cause of individual differences, since we know that any continued pressure from without awakens an adaptive response in the form of the vegetable organism.

III. The Choice and Fixation of Variations.

We have now seen that every living object is unlike every other. In plants, even every branch is unlike any other branch. We have endeavored to discover some of the causes of these universal differences. We have found that they are intimately associated with the welfare of the type or species, inasmuch as they appear, for the most part, to be the means of fitting the plant to live in the conditions in which it is placed. But we have also seen that there are more individuals than can find a place to live. How, then, does nature choose the best from the poorest, and, having chosen them, how does she endeavor to fix them, or to make them more or less stable?

"This preservation of favorable individual differences and variations, and the destruction of those which are injurious, I have called Natural Selection or the Survival of the Fittest." This is the philosophy which was propounded by Darwin, and which will carry his name to the last generation of men. It looks simple enough. Those forms which are best fitted to live, do live, because they crowd out the others. Yet, this simple principle of natural selection was the first explanation of the process of evolution which seemed to be capable of interpreting the complex phenomena of the forms of organic life. For a time, this philosophy was thought to be the one fundamental motive of the evolution or progression of life, but we are now convinced that there are other motives or forces at work; but it seems to be indisputable that natural selection is the chief force underlying the evolution of plants, and it is the only one with which the person who desires to breed plants need intimately concern himself.

We must now determine what a variety is. This is a vexed question, and one which seems never to be capable of an answer which is satisfactory to the gardener. Time and again, some person has introduced what he considered to be a distinct new variety, only to find that other horticulturists dispute him and declare that it is only some old variety renamed. And yet the introducer knows that he has not renamed an old variety, but that he has simply propagated a form which appeared or originated upon his own grounds.

Now, let us see. Nature starts out with the individual to make a new form. Every individual is unlike every other one. When the individual differences are so well marked that we can readily describe and distinguish them, and so permanent that they pass down nearly intact to a few generations, we say that we have a variety. If the differences are still more marked, we say that we have a species. Where the variety ends and the species begins it may be utterly impossible to determine; so we mark off at a certain point and say, arbitrarily, that this much is variety and that much is species. Asa Gray once said to me that "species are judgments." Now, if there is no hard and fast line between the variety and the species, so there is none between the individual and the variety; for a variety is only the family of descendants from some one individual. That is, the idea of variety or species rests upon difference, but just how much difference shall constitute one grade or another is a matter of individual opinion. So, when two gardeners cannot agree as to whether a given introduction is a new variety or not, they are having just the same difficulty that two botanists have when they cannot decide whether two plants are two species or one.

It is apparent, then, that every individual plant is a distinct variety, only that the differences between it and other individuals may be so slight that they have no practical utility and cannot be described and recorded. Just as soon as an individual plant has characters so unlike its kin that it has some commercial value, then the plant will be increased by cuttings or grafts or seeds, the brood of offspring will be given a name, and a new variety is born.

Individuals with the same general features may appear simultaneously in two or more places, and two or more men may propagate, name, and introduce them. When they are all brought together and compared, it will be said that they are all the same variety, that, according to the rules of nomenclature, the brood which chanced to be named first must "stand" or be held to be the type of the variety, and that the other names must become synonyms. Yet some person may discover minor differences in them and demand that the varieties be kept distinct. So the see-saw goes on — a variety is a variety so long as it answers some purpose in use or trade, and it is not a variety when it is so much like some other variety that it has no merit which the other does not possess.

As soon as a plant appears with some feature which is more desirable than anything which has preceded it, therefore, it may be made the beginning of a new variety. Man chooses it, and then propagates it. This is human selection. If nature did the same, it would be natural selection.

Now, how does nature preserve or fix this type? She does not preserve it! She simply chooses it as a beginning and gradually modifies it and shapes it into the form which she needs. She has no permanent forms. There is a general onward progression of every type either towards other types or towards extinction. We have seen that nature is constantly choosing and selecting. If she selects an individual for the beginning of a race, then she selects just as keenly from every offspring of that individual, and so on to the end of time. The process never stops. So nature fixes her forms by keeping them moving, growing, constantly developing farther away from their beginnings.

Now, man does the same thing. A plant in a cabbage row pleases him. It has a solid, small head and stout stem. He stores it away for seed. Amongst the offspring, perhaps fifty per cent are as good as the parent. These are saved. So the process goes on, from season to season. In four or five generations of plants, he finds that ninety per cent of the seeds "come true." Then he names it and introduces it. It is well advertised in the seed catalogues. Many people buy the seeds. Some of these persons will grow their own seed, and every one of them has a different ideal in mind when selecting the seed parents. So, in the course of a few years, it is found that there are really several more or less different forms going under the same name. Some person may observe this difference and legitimately introduce one or more of the forms as distinct varieties. Some other person, however, who has known the history of the stock and who is not aware that varieties pass into other forms, objects to the new names and declares that the introducer is imposing upon the public.

This is the history of ninety-nine out of every hundred varieties which are habitually propagated by seeds, like the kitchen-garden vegetables and the annual flowers. Some peculiar individual, appearing we know not why, is discovered, and seeds are saved and selection — perhaps unconscious selection — begins. After a time the variety is broken up into several, or else, if it varies only slightly into divergent forms, the whole body or generations of the variety move onward, gradually departing from the initial type until it is no longer the same, although it may still bear the same name. The life of seed-varieties, in their pure and original form, is very short. Even the best of them are usually measured by one or two decades. They run out or pass out by variation, into other forms. The Trophy tomato is not the Trophy tomato which was introduced over twenty years ago, although it bears the old name and is a direct descendant of the first stock.

In plants multiplied by buds — that is, by budding, grafting, cuttings, tubers, and the like — there is less variation in the offspring than in those propagated by seeds. Yet we have seen that no two Baldwin apple trees — all of which are but divisions, more or less remote, of the one original tree — are alike, and now and then one branch of a fruit tree may "sport," or develop a strange bud-variety. We know, too, that the same variety of fruit tree takes on different characters in different geographical regions, so that the Greening apple is no longer the Greening of Rhode Island in the West and South. So, it is apparent that even when we divide a plant into many parts and distribute the members far and wide, and when there is no occasion for concerning ourselves with fixing the type, — even here there is variation. In some cases, particularly in those in which we multiply the plant by dividing abnormally developed parts, there is a tendency to scatter or to vary in many directions, and also a tendency to run out by degeneration. This is admirably true of the potato, varieties of which, in ten years or less, become so mixed in their characters, through rapid variation and deterioration, that we must return to seedling productions for a new start.

The gist of all this is the fact that nature does not make new varieties or species by leaps and bounds or sudden starts, but that she gradually produces the new out of the old, so slowly that were a man to live a thousand years he might note little change in the grosser features of plants. She employs crossing, the changes in all the varied conditions of life, and whatever other forces she may possess, to give small differences between individuals. Then the slow and cumulative process of selection carries the work forward forever. Man must follow the same course, in the main. He is only rarely the direct means of originating variations. He finds them amongst the normal plants of the field and garden. His skill and science are exercised in the selection and so-called breeding of the offspring, not in the original genesis of the new form. It is only in those plants which he multiplies by simple division that he gains much direct profit by crossing or hybridizing. It is the slow and patient care and selection, day by day, which permanently ameliorate and improve the vegetable world. Nature starts the work; man may complete it.

LECTURE II.

THE PHILOSOPHY OF THE CROSSING OF PLANTS, CONSIDERED IN REFERENCE TO THEIR IMPROVEMENT UNDER CULTIVATION.

I. THE STRUGGLE FOR LIFE.

It is now understood that the specific forms or groups of plants have been determined largely by the survival of the fittest in a long and severe struggle for existence. The proof that this struggle everywhere exists becomes evident upon a moment's reflection. We know that all organisms are eminently variable. In fact, no two plants or animals in the world are exactly alike. We also know that very few of the whole number of seeds which are produced in any area ever grow into plants. If all the seeds produced by the elms upon Boston Common in any fruitful year were to grow into trees, this city would become a forest as a result. If all the seeds of the rarest orchid in our woods were to grow, in a few generations of plants even our farms would be overrun. If all the rabbits which are born were to reach old age, and all their offspring were to do the same, in less than ten years every vestige of herbage would be swept from the country, and our farms would become barren. There is, then, a wonderful latent potency in these species; but the same may be said of every species of plant and animal, even of man himself. If one species of plant would overrun and usurp the land if it increased to the full extent of its possibilities, what would be the result if each of the two thousand and sixty-one plants known to inhabit Middlesex County were to do the same? And then fancy the result if each of the animals, from rabbits and mice to frogs and leeches, were to increase without check! The plagues of Egypt would be insignificant in the comparison!

The fact is, the world is not big enough to hold the possible first offspring of the plants and animals at this moment living upon it. Struggle for existence, then, is inevitable, and it must be severe. It follows as a necessity that those seeds grow or those plants live which are best fitted to grow and live, or which are fortunate enough to find a congenial foothold. It would appear, at first thought, that much depends upon the accident of falling into a congenial place, or one unoccupied by other plants or animals; but, inasmuch as scores of plants are contending for every unoccupied place, it follows that everywhere only the fittest can germinate or grow. In the great majority of cases, plants grow in a certain place because they are better fitted to grow there, to hold their own, than any other plants are; and the instances are rare in which a plant is so fortunate as to find an unoccupied place. We are apt to think that plants chance to grow where we find them, but the chance is determined by law, and therefore is not chance.

Much of the capability of a plant to persist under all this struggle depends, therefore, upon how much it varies; for the more it varies the more likely it is to find places of least struggle. It grows under various conditions, — in sun and shade, in sand and clay, by the sea-shore or upon the hills, in the humidity of the forest or the aridity of the plain. In some directions it very likely finds less struggle than in others, and in these directions it expands itself, multiplies, and gradually dies out in other directions. So it happens that it tends to take on new forms, or to undergo an evolution. In the meantime, all the intermediate forms, which are at best only indifferently adapted to their conditions, tend to disappear. In other words, gaps appear which we call " missing links." The weak links break and fall away, and what was once a chain becomes a series of rings. So the " missing links " are amongst the best proofs of evolution.

The question now arises as to the cause of these numerous variations in animals and plants. Why are no two individuals in nature exactly alike? The question is exceedingly difficult to answer.

It was once said that plants vary because it is their nature to vary; that variation is a necessary function, as much as growth or fructification. This really removes the question beyond the reach of philosophy; and direct observation leads us to think that some variation, at least, is due to external circumstances. (See Lecture I.) We are now looking for the cause of variation as a part of the scheme of evolution; and we are wondering if the varied surroundings, or, as Darwin put it, the "changed conditions of life," may not actually induce variability. This conclusion would seem to follow from the fact of the severe and universal struggle in nature whereby plants are constantly forced into new and strange conditions. But there is undoubtedly much variation which has sprung from more remote causes, one of which it is my purpose to discuss here.

II. The Division of Labor.

In the lowest animals and plants — which are simply single cells — the species multiplies by means of simple division or by budding. One individual, of itself, becomes two, and the two are therefore recasts of the one. But, as organisms multiplied and conditions became more complex, that is, as struggle increased, there came a differentiation in the parts of the individual, so that one cell or one cluster of cells performed one labor and other cells performed other labor; and this tendency resulted in the development of organs. Simple division, therefore, could no longer reproduce the whole complex individual; and, as all organs are necessary to the existence of life, the organism may die if it is divided. Along with this specialization came the differentiation into sex; and sex clearly has two offices: to hand over, by some mysterious process, the complex organization of the parent to the offspring, and also to unite the essential characters or tendencies of two beings into one. The second office is manifestly the greater, for, as it unites two organizations into one, it insures that the offspring is somewhat unlike either parent, and is therefore better fitted to seize upon any place or condition new to its kind. And as the generations increase, the tendency to variation in the offspring must be constantly greater, because the impressions of a greater number of ancestors are transmitted to it. I have said that this office of sex to induce variation is more important than the mere fact of reproduction of a complex organization; for it must be borne in mind that the complexity of organization is itself a variation and adaptation made necessary by the increasing struggle for existence.

If, therefore, the philosophy of sex is to promote variation by the union of different individuals, it must follow that the greatest variation must come from parents considerably unlike each other in their minor characters. Thus it comes that inbreeding tends to weaken a type, and cross-breeding tends to strengthen it. And at this point we meet the particular subject which I am to present to you. I have introduced you to this preliminary sketch because I contend that we can understand crossing only as we make it a part of the general philosophy of nature. There are the vaguest notions concerning the possibilities of crossing, some of which I hope to correct by presenting the subject in its relations to the general aspects of the vegetable world.

We are now prepared to understand that crossing is good for the species, because it constantly revitalizes offspring with the strongest traits of the parents, and ever presents new combinations which enable the individuals to stand a better chance of securing a place in the polity of nature. The further discussions of the subject are such as have to do with the extent to which crossing is possible and advisable, and the general results of the operation.

III. The Limits of Crossing.

If crossing is good for the species, which philosophy and direct experiment abundantly show, it is necessary at once to find out to what extent it can be carried. Does the good increase in proportion as the cross becomes more violent, or as the parents are more and more unlike? Or do we soon find a limit beyond which it is not profitable or even possible to go,—a point at which we say that "an inch is as good as an ell"? If great variability is good for the species in the struggle for existence, and if crossing induces variability because of the union of unlike individuals, it would seem to follow that the more unlike the parents are, the greater will be the variation in offspring and the more the type will prosper; and, carrying this thought to its logical conclusion, we should expect to find that the most closely related plants would constantly tend to refuse to cross, because the offspring of them would be little variable and therefore little adapted to the struggle for existence; while the most widely separated plants would constantly tend to cross more and more, because their offspring would present the greatest possible degrees of differences. We should expect, for instance, that a Baldwin apple would be less likely to cross with a Greening than it is to cross with a peach or a gourd. And, if we should carry our thought a step farther, we should at once see that this crossing between different species would soon fill in all differences between those species, and that definite specific types would cease to exist. This would be pandemonium, and crossing would be the cause of it!

Now, essentially this reasoning has been advanced to combat the evolution of plants and animals by means of natural selection; and this proposition that intermixing must constantly tend to obliterate all differences between plants and to prevent the establishment of well-marked types, has been called the "swamping effects of intercrossing." It is exceedingly important that we consider this question, for it really lies at the foundation of the improvement of cultivated plants by means of crossing, as well as the persistence and evolution of varieties and species under wholly natural conditions.

We find, however, that distinct species, as a rule, refuse to cross; and the first question which naturally arises is, What is the immediate cause of the refusal of plants to cross? How does this refusal express itself? It comes about in many ways. The commonest cause is the positive refusal of a plant to allow its ovules to be impregnated by the pollen of another plant. The pollen will not "take." For instance, if we apply the pollen of a Hubbard squash to the flower of the common field pumpkin, there will simply be no result,— the fruit will not form. The same is true of the pear and the apple, the oat and the wheat, and most very unlike species. Or the refusal may come in the sterility of the cross or hybrid: the pollen may "take" and seeds may be formed and the seeds may grow, but the plants which they produce may be wholly barren, sometimes even refusing to produce flowers as well as seeds, as in the instance of some hybrids between the Wild Goose plum and the peach. Sometimes the refusal to cross is due to some difference in the time of blooming or some incompatibility in the structure of the flowers. But it is enough for our purpose to know that there are certain characters in widely dissimilar plants which prevent intercrossing, and that these characters are just as positive and just as much influenced by change of environment and natural selection as are size, color, productiveness, and other characters.

Here, then, is the sufficient answer to the proposition that intercrossing must swamp all natural selection, and also the explanation of the varying and often restricted limits within which crossing is possible. That is, the checks to crossing have been developed through the principle of universal variability and natural selection, as has been shown by Darwin and Wallace. Plants vary in their reproductive organs and powers just the same as they do in other directions; and when such a variation is useful it is perpetuated, and when hurtful it is lost. Suppose that a certain well-marked individual of a species should find an unusually good place in nature, and it should multiply rapidly. Crosses would be made between its own offspring and perhaps between those offspring and itself in succeeding years; and it is fair to suppose that some of the crosses would be particularly well adapted to the conditions in which the parent grew, and these would constantly tend to perpetuate themselves, while less adaptive forms would constantly tend to disappear. Now, the same thing would take place if this individual or its adaptive offspring were to cross with the main stock of the parent species; for all the offspring of such a cross which are intermediate in character and therefore less adapted to the new conditions would tend to disappear, and the two types would, as a result, become more and more fixed and the tendency to cross would constantly decrease.

The refusal to cross, therefore, becomes a positive character of separation, and the "missing links" which result from crossing are no more or no less inexplicable than the "missing links" due to simple selection; or, to put the case more accurately, natural selection weeds out the tendency to promiscuous crossing, when it is hurtful, in just the same manner that it weeds out any other injurious tendency. It makes no difference in what way this tendency expresses itself, whether in some constitutional refusal to cross, — if such exists, — or in infertility of offspring, or in different times of blooming: all equally come under the power of natural selection. We are apt to look upon infertility as the absence of a character, a sort of a negative feature which is somehow not the legitimate property of natural selection; but such is not the case. We are perhaps led the more to this feeling because the word infertility is itself negative, and because we associate full productiveness with the positive attributes of plants. But loss of productiveness is surely no more a subject of wonder than loss of color or size, if there is some corresponding gain to be accomplished. In fact, we see, in numerous plants which propagate easily by means of runners and suckers, a very low degree of productiveness, that is, infertility.

Now, if this reasoning is sound, it leads us to conclusions quite the reverse of those held by the advocates of the swamping effects of intercrossing, and these conclusions are of the most vital importance to every man who tills the soil. The logical result is simply this: the best results of crossing are obtained, as a rule, when the cross is made between different individuals of the same variety, or at farthest, between different individuals of the same species. In other words, hybrids — or crosses between species — are rarely useful in nature, and it follows that the more unlike the species the less useful will be the hybrids. This, I am aware, is counter to the notions of most horticulturists, and, if true, must entirely overthrow our common thinking upon this subject. But I think that I shall be able to show that observation and experiment lead to the same conclusion to which our philosophy has brought us.

IV. Function of the Cross.

a. *The Gradual Amelioration of the Type.*

At this point we must ask ourselves what we mean by "best results." I take this phrase to refer to those plants which are best fitted to survive in the struggle for existence, those which are most vigorous or most productive or most hardy, or which possess any well-marked character or characters which distinguish them in virility from their fellows. We commonly associate the term more particularly with marked vigor and productiveness; these are the characters most useful in nature and also in cultivation, the ones which we oftenest desire to obtain. Another type of variation which we constantly covet is something which we can call a new character, which will lead to the production of a new cultural variety, and we are always looking to this as the legitimate result of crossing. We have forgotten — if, indeed, we ever knew — that the commoner, all-pervading, more important function of the cross is to infuse some new strength or power into the offspring, to improve or to perpetuate an existing variety, rather than to create a new one. Or, if a new one is created, it comes from the gradual passing of one into another, an inferior variety into a good one, a good one into a superlative one. So nature employs crossing in a process of slow or gradual improvement, one step leading to another, and not in any bold or sudden creation of new forms. And there is evidence to show that something akin to this must be done to secure the best and most permanent results under cultivation. The notion is somehow firmly rooted in the popular mind that new varieties can be produced with the greatest ease by crossing parents of given attributes. There is something captivating about the notion. It smacks of a somewhat magic power which man evokes as he passes his wand over the untamed forces of nature. But the wand is often only a gilded stick, and is apt to serve no better purpose than the drum major's pretentious baton!

Let me say further that crossing alone can accomplish comparatively little. The chief power in the evolution or progression of plants appears to be selection, or, as Darwin puts it, the law of "preservation of favorable individual differences and variations, and the destruction of those which are injurious." Selection is the force which augments, develops, and fixes types. Man must not only practice a judicious selection of parents from which the cross is to come, which is in reality but the exercise of a choice, but he must constantly select the best from among the crosses, in order to maintain a high degree of usefulness and to make any advancement; and it sometimes happens that the selection is much more important to the cultivator than the crossing. I do not wish to discourage the crossing of plants, but I do desire to dispel the charm which too often hangs about it.

Further discussion of this subject naturally falls under two heads: the improvement of existing types or varieties by means of crossing, and the summary production of new varieties. I have already stated that the former office is the more important one, and the proposition is easy of proof. It is the chief use which nature makes of crossing, — to strengthen the type. Think, for instance, of the great rarity of hybrids or pronounced crosses in nature. No doubt all the authentic cases on record could be entered in one or two volumes, but a list of all the individual plants of the world could not be compressed into ten thousand volumes. There are a few genera, in which the species are not well defined or in which some character of inflorescence favors promiscuous crossing, in which hybrids are conspicuous; but even here the number of individual hybrids is very small in comparison to the whole number of individuals. That is, the hybrids are rare, while the parents may be common. This is well illustrated even in the willows and oaks, in which, perhaps, hybrids are better known than in any other American plants. The great genus carex or sedge, which occurs in great numbers and many species in almost every locality in New England, and in which the species are particularly adapted to intercrossing by the character of their inflorescence, furnishes but few undoubted hybrids. Among one hundred and eighty-five species and prominent varieties inhabiting the northeastern states, there are only eleven hybrids recorded, and all of them are rare or local, some of them having been collected but once. Species of carex of remarkable similarity may grow side by side for years, even intertangled in the same clump, and yet produce no hybrid. These instances prove that nature avoids hybridization, — a conclusion at which we have already arrived from philosophical considerations. And we have reason to infer the same conclusion from the fact that flowers of different species are so constructed as not to invite intercrossing. But, on the other hand, the fact that all higher plants habitually propagate by means of seeds, which is far the most expensive to the plant of all methods of propagation, while at the same time most flowers are so constructed as to prevent self-fertilization, proves that some corresponding good must come from crossing within the limits of the species or variety; and there are purely philosophical reasons, as we have seen, which warrant a similar conclusion.

But experiment has given us more direct proof of our propositions, and we shall now turn our attention to the garden.

Darwin was the first to show that crossing within the limits of the species or variety results in a constant revitalizing of the offspring, and that this is the particular ultimate function of cross-fertilization. Kölreuter, Sprengel, Knight, and others had observed many, if, indeed, not all, the facts obtained by Darwin; but they had not generalized upon them broadly, and did not conceive their relation to the complex life of the vegetable world. Darwin's results are, concisely, these; self-fertilization tends to weaken the offspring; crossing between different plants of the same variety gives stronger and more productive offspring than arises from self-fertilization; crossing between stocks of the same variety grown in different places or under different conditions gives better offspring than crossing between different plants grown in the same place or under similar conditions; and his researches have also shown that, as a rule, flowers are so constructed as to favor cross-fertilization. In short, he found, as he expressed it, that "nature abhors perpetual self-fertilization." Some of his particular results, although often quoted, will be useful in fixing these facts in our minds. Plants from crossed seeds of morning-glory exceeded in height those from self-fertilized seeds as 100 exceeds

76, in the first generation. Some flowers from these plants were self-pollinated and some were crossed, and in this second generation the crossed plants were to the uncrossed as 100 is to 79; the operation was again repeated, and in the third generation the figures stand 100 to 68; fourth generation, the plants having been grown in midwinter, when none of them did well, 100 to 86; fifth generation, 100 to 75; sixth generation, 100 to 72; seventh generation, 100 to 81; eighth generation, 100 to 85; ninth generation, 100 to 79; tenth generation, 100 to 54. The average total gain in height of the crossed over the uncrossed was as 100 to 77, or about 30 per cent. There was a corresponding gain in fertility, or the number of seeds and seed-pods produced. Yet, striking as the results are, they were produced by simply crossing between plants grown near together, and under what would ordinarily be called uniform conditions. In order to determine the influence of crossing with fresh stock, plants of the same variety were obtained from another garden, and these were crossed with the ninth generation mentioned above. The offspring of this cross exceeded those of the other crossed plants as 100 exceeds 78, in height; as 100 exceeds 57, in the number of seed-pods; and as 100 exceeds 51, in the weight of the seed-pods. In other words, crosses between fresh stock of the same variety were nearly 30 per cent more vigorous than crosses between plants grown side by side for some time and over 44 per cent more vigorous than plants from self-fertilized seeds. On the other hand, experiments showed that crosses between different flowers upon the same plant gave actually poorer results than offspring of self-fertilized flowers. It is evident, from all these figures, that nature desires crosses between plants, and, if possible, between plants grown under somewhat different conditions. All the results are exceedingly interesting and important; and there is every reason to believe that, as a rule, similar results can be obtained with all plants.

Darwin extended his investigations to many plants, only a few of which need be discussed here. Cabbage gave pronounced results. Crossed plants were to self-fertilized plants in weight as 100 is to 37. A cross was now made between these crossed plants and a plant of the same variety from another garden, and the difference in weight of the resulting offspring was the difference between 100 and 22, showing a gain of over 350 per cent, due to a cross with fresh stock. Crossed lettuce plants exceeded uncrossed in height as 100 exceeds 82. Buckwheat gave an increase in weight of seeds as 100 to 82, and in height of plants as 100 to 69. Beets gave an increase in height represented by 100 and 87. Maize, when full grown, from crossed and uncrossed seeds, gave the differences in height between 100 and 91. Canary-grass gave similar results.

I have obtained results as well marked as these upon a large and what might be called a commercial scale. I raised the plants during the first generation of seeds from known parentage, the flowers from which they came having been carefully pollinated by hand. In some instances the second generations were grown from hand-crossed seeds, but in other cases the second generations were grown from seeds simply selected from the first-year patches. As the experiments have been made in the field and upon a somewhat extensive scale, it was not possible to accurately measure the plants and the fruits from individuals in all cases; but the results have been so marked as to admit of no doubt as to their character. In 1889 several hand-crosses were made among egg-plants. Three fruits matured, and the seeds from them were grown in 1890. Some two hundred plants were grown, and they were characterized throughout the season by great sturdiness and vigor of growth. They grew more erect and taller than other plants near by grown from commercial seeds. They were the finest plants which I had ever seen. It was impossible to determine productiveness, from the fact that our seasons are too short for egg-plants, and only the earliest flowers, in the large varieties, perfect their fruit, and the plant blooms continuously through the season. In order to determine how much a plant will bear, it must be grown until it ceases to bloom. When frost came, I could see little difference in productiveness between these crossed plants and commercial plants. A dozen fruits were selected from various parts of this patch, and in 1891 about twenty-five hundred plants were grown from them. Again the plants were remarkably robust and healthy, with fine foliage, and they grew erect and tall, — an indication of vigor. They were also very productive; but, as the cross had been made between unlike varieties, and the offsprings were therefore unlike either parent, I could not make an accurate comparison. But they compared well with commercial egg-plants, and I am satisfied that they would have shown themselves to be more productive than common stock could they have grown a month or six weeks longer. Professor Munson, of the Maine Agricultural College, grew some of this crossed stock in 1891, and he told me that it was better than any commercial stock in his gardens.

In extended experiments in the crossing of pumpkins, squashes, and gourds, carried on during several years, increase in productiveness due to crossing has been marked in many instances. Marked increase in productiveness has been obtained from tomato crosses, even when no other results of crossing could be seen.

b. *Change of Seed and Crossing.*

Bearing in mind these good influences of crossing, let us recall another series of facts following the simple change of seed. Almost every farmer and gardener at the present day feel that an occasional change of seed results in better crops, and there are definite records to show that such is often the case. In fact, I am convinced that much of the rapid improvement in fruits and vegetables in recent years is due to the practice of buying plants and seeds so largely of dealers, by means of which the stock is often changed. Even a slight change, as between farms or neighboring villages, sometimes produces marked results, such as more vigorous plants and often more fruitful ones. We must not suppose, however, that because a small change gives a good result, a violent or very pronounced change gives a better one. There are many facts on record to show that great changes often profoundly influence plants, and when such influence results in lessened vigor or lessened productiveness we call it an injurious one. Now, this injurious influence may result even when all the conditions in the new place are favorable to the health and development of the plant; it is an influence which is wholly independent, so far as we can see, of any condition which interferes injuriously with the simple processes of growth. Seeds of a native physalis or husk-tomato were sent to me from Paraguay in 1889 by Dr. Thomas Morong, then travelling in that country. I grew it both in the house and out of doors, and for two generations was unable to make it set fruit, even though the flowers were hand-pollinated; yet the plants were healthy and grew vigorously. The third generation grown out of doors set fruit freely. This is an instance of the fact that very great changes of conditions may injuriously affect the plant, and an equally good illustration of the power to overcome these conditions. Now, there is great similarity between the effects of slight and violent changes of conditions and small and violent degrees of crossing, as both Darwin and Wallace have pointed out, and it is pertinent to this discussion to endeavor to discover why this similarity exists.

It is well proved that crossing is good for the resulting offspring, because the differences between the parents carry over new combinations of characters or at least new powers into the crosses. It is a process of revitalization, and the more different the stocks in desirable characters within the limits of the variety, the greater is the revitalization; and frequently the good is of a more positive kind, resulting in pronounced characters which may serve as the basis for new varieties. In the cross, therefore, a new combination of characters or a new power fit it to live better than its parents in the conditions under which they lived.

In the case of change of stock we find just the reverse, which, however, amounts to the same thing, — that the same characters or powers fit the plant to live better in conditions new to it than plants which have long lived in those conditions. In either case, the good comes from the fitting together of new characters or powers and new environments. Plants which live during many generations in one place become accustomed to the place, thoroughly fitted into its conditions, and are in what Mr. Spencer calls a state of equilibrium. When either plant or conditions change, new adjustments must take place; and the plant may find an opportunity to take advantage, to expand in some direction in which it has before been held back; for plants always possess greater power than they are able to express. "These rhythmical actions or functions [of the organism]," writes Spencer, "and the various compound rhythms resulting from their combinations, are in such adjustment as to balance the actions to which the organism is subject. There is a constant or periodic genesis of forces which, in their kinds, amounts, and directions, suffice to antagonize the forces which the organism has constantly or periodically to bear. If, then, there exists this state of moving equilibrium among a definite set of internal actions, exposed to a definite set of external actions, what must result if any of the external actions are changed? Of course there is no longer an equilibrium. Some force which the organism habitually generates is too great or too small to balance some incident force; and there arises a residuary force exerted by the environment on the organism, or by the organism on the environment. This residuary force, this unbalanced force, of necessity expends itself in producing some change of state in the organism."

The good results, therefore, are processes of adaptation, and when adaptation is perfectly complete the plant may have gained no permanent advantage over its former condition, and new crossing or another change may be necessary; yet there is often a permanent gain, as when a plant becomes visibly modified by change to another climate. Now, this adaptive change may express itself in two ways: either by some direct influence upon the stature, vigor, or other general character, or indirectly upon the reproductive powers, by which some new influence is carried to the offspring. If the direct influences become hereditary, as observation seems to show may sometimes occur, the two directions of modification may amount, ultimately, to the same thing.

For the purposes of this discussion it is enough

to know that crossing within the variety and change of stock within ordinary bounds are beneficial, that the results in the two cases seem to flow from essentially the same causes, and that crossing and change of stock combined give much better results than either one alone; and this benefit is expressed more in increased yield and vigor than in novel and striking variations. These processes are much more important than any mere groping after new varieties, as I have already said; not only because they are surer, but because they are universal and necessary means of maintaining and improving both wild and cultivated plants. Even after one succeeds in securing and fixing a new variety, he must employ these means to a greater or less extent to maintain fertility and vigor, and to keep the variety true to its type. In the case of some garden crops, in which many seeds are produced in each fruit and in which the operation of pollination is easy, actual hand-crossing from new stock now and then may be found to be profitable. But in most cases the operation can be left to nature, if the new stock is planted among the old. Upon this point Darwin expressed himself as follows: " It is a common practice with horticulturists to obtain seeds from another place having a very different soil, so as to avoid raising plants for a long succession of generations under the same conditions; but with all the species which freely intercross by the aid of insects or the wind, it would be an incomparably better plan to obtain seeds of the required variety, which had been raised for some generations under as different conditions as possible, and sow them in alternate rows with seeds matured in the old garden. The two stocks would then intercross, with a thorough blending of their whole organizations, and with no loss of purity to the variety, and this would yield far more favorable results than a mere change of seed."

c. *The Outright Production of New Varieties.*

But you are waiting for a discussion of the second of the great features of crossing,—the summary production of new varieties. This is the subject which is almost universally associated with crossing in the popular mind, and even among horticulturists themselves. It is the commonest notion that the desirable characters of given parents can be definitely combined in a pronounced cross or hybrid. There are two or three philosophical reasons which somewhat oppose this doctrine, and which we will do well to consider at the outset. In the first place, nature is opposed to hybrids, for species have been bred away from each other in the ability to cross. If, therefore, there is no advantage for nature to hybridize, we may suppose that there would be little advantage for man to do so; and there would be no advantage for man did he not place the plant under conditions different from nature, or desire a different set of characters. We have seen that nature's chief barriers to hybridization are total refusal of species to unite, and entire or comparative seedlessness of offspring. We can overcome the refusal to cross in many cases by bringing the plant under cultivation; for the character of the species becomes so changed by the wholly new conditions that its former antipathies may be overpowered. Yet it is doubtful if such a plant will ever acquire a complete willingness to cross. In like manner we can overcome in a measure the comparative seedlessness of hybrids, but it is very doubtful if we can ever make such hybrids completely fruitful. It would appear, therefore, upon theoretical grounds, that in plants in which seeds are the parts sought, no good can be expected, as a rule, from hybridization; and this seems to be affirmed by facts.[1]

It is evident that species which have been differentiated or bred away from each other in a given locality will have more opposed qualities or powers than similar species which have arisen quite independently in places remote from each

[1] See definition of hybrids, crosses, and other terms in the Glossary.

other. In the one case the species have likely struggled with each other until each one has attained to a degree of divergence which allows it to persist; while in the other case there has been no struggle between the species, but similar conditions have brought about similar results. These similar species which appear independently of each other in different places are called representative species. Islands remote from each other but similarly situated with reference to climate very often contain representative species; and the same may be said of other regions much like each other, as eastern North America and Japan. Now, it follows that, if representative species are less opposed than others, they are more likely to hybridize with good results; and this fact is remarkably well illustrated in the Kieffer and allied pears, which are hybrids between representative species of Europe and Japan; and I am inclined to think that the same may be found to be true of the common or European apple and the wild crab of the Mississippi valley. Various crabs of the Soulard type, which I once thought to constitute a distinct species, appear upon further study to be hybrids. We will also recall that the hybrid grapes which have so far proved most valuable are those obtained by Rogers between the American Vitis Labrusca and the European wine grape; and that the attempts of Haskell and others to hybridize associated species of native grapes have given, at best, only indifferent results. To these good results from hybrids of fruit trees and vines I shall revert presently.

Another theoretical point, which is borne out by practice, is the conclusion that, because of the great differences and lack of affinity between parents, pronounced hybrid offsprings are unstable. This is one of the greatest difficulties in the way of the summary production of new varieties by means of hybridization. It would appear, also, that, because of the unlikeness of parents, hybrid offspring must be exceedingly variable; but, as a matter of fact, in many instances the parents are so pronouncedly different that the hybrids represent a distinct type by themselves, or else they approach very nearly to the characters of one of the parents. There are, to be sure, many instances of exceedingly variable hybrid offspring, but they are usually the offspring of variable parents. In other words, variability in offspring appears to follow rather as a result of variability in parents than as a result of mere unlikeness of characters. But the instability of hybrid offspring when propagated by seed is notorious. Wallace writes that "the effect of occasional crosses often results in a great amount of variation, but it also leads to instability of character, and is therefore very little employed in the production of fixed and well-marked races." I may remark again that, because of the unequal and unknown powers of the parents, we can never predict what characters will appear in the hybrids. This fact was well expressed by Lindley a half century ago, in the phrase, "Hybridizing is a game of chance played between man and plants."

V. Characteristics of Crosses.

Bearing these fundamental propositions in mind, let us pursue the subject somewhat in detail. We shall find that the characters of hybrids, as compared with the characters of simple crosses between stocks of the same variety, are ambiguous, negative, and often prejudicial. The fullest discussion of hybrids has been made by Focke (see Lecture IV.), and he lays down the five following propositions concerning the character of hybrid offspring:—

1. "All individuals which have come from the crossing of two pure species or races, when produced and grown under like conditions, are usually exactly like each other, or at least scarcely more different from each other than plants of the same species are." This proposition, although perhaps true in the main, appears to be too broadly and positively stated.

2. "The characters of hybrids may be different

from the characters of the parents. The hybrids differ most in size and vigor and in their sexual powers."

3. "Hybrids are distinguished from their parents by their powers of vegetation or growth. Hybrids between very different species are often weak, especially when young, so that it is difficult to raise them. On the other hand, cross-breeds are, as a rule, uncommonly vigorous; they are distinguished mostly by size, rapidity of growth, early flowering, productiveness, longer life, stronger reproductive power, unusual size of some special organs, and similar characteristics."

4. "Hybrids produce a less amount of pollen and fewer seeds than their parents, and they often produce none. In cross-breeds this weakening of the reproductive powers does not occur. The flowers of sterile or nearly sterile hybrids usually remain fresh a long time."

5. "Malformations and odd forms are apt to appear in hybrids, especially in the flowers."

Some of the relations between hybridization and crossing within narrow limits are stated as follows by Darwin: "It is an extraordinary fact that with many species flowers fertilized with their own pollen are either absolutely or in some degree sterile; if fertilized with pollen from another flower on the same plant, they are sometimes, though rarely, a little more fertile; if fertilized with pollen from another individual or variety of the same species, they are fully fertile; but if with pollen from a distinct species, they are sterile in all possible degrees, until utter sterility is reached. We thus have a long series with absolute sterility at the two ends; at one end due to the sexual elements not having been sufficiently differentiated, and at the other end to their having been differentiated in too great a degree, or in some peculiar manner."

The difficulties in the way of successful results through hybridization are, therefore, these: the difficulty of effecting the cross; infertility, instability, variability, and often weakness and monstrosity of the hybrids; and the absolute impossibility of predicting results. The advantage to be derived from a successful hybridization is the securing of a new variety which shall combine in some measure the most desirable features of both parents; and this advantage is often of so great moment that it is worth while to make repeated efforts and to overlook numerous failures. From these theoretical considerations it is apparent that hybridization is essentially an empirical subject, and the results are such as fall under the common denomination of chance. And, as it does not rest upon any legitimate function in nature, we can understand that it will always be difficult to codify laws upon it.

Among the various characters of hybrid offspring, I presume that the most prejudicial one is their instability, their tendency still to vary into new forms or to return to one or the other parent in succeeding generations. It is difficult to fix any particular form which we may secure in the first generation of hybrids. At the outset, we notice that this discouraging feature is manifested chiefly through the fact of seed-reproduction, and we thereby come upon what is perhaps the most important practical consideration in hybridization, — the fact that the great majority of the best hybrids in cultivation are increased by bud-propagation, as cuttings, layers, suckers, buds, or grafts. In fact, I recall very few instances in this country of good undoubted hybrids which are propagated with practical certainty by means of seeds. You will recall that the genera in which hybrids are most common are those in which bud-propagation is the rule; as begonia, pelargonium, orchids, gladiolus, rhododendron, roses, cannas, and the fruits. This simply means that it is difficult to fix hybrids so that they will come "true to seed," and makes apparent the fact that if we desire hybrids we must expect to propagate them by means of buds.

This is a point which appears to have been overlooked by those who contend that hybridization must necessarily swamp all results of natural selection; for, as comparatively few plants propagate habitually by means of buds, whatever hybrids might have appeared would have been speedily lost, and all the more, also, because, by the terms of their reasoning, the hybrids would cross with other and dissimilar forms, and therefore lose their identity as intermediates. Or, starting with the assumption that hybrids are intermediates, and would therefore obliterate specific types, we must conclude that they should have some marked degree of stability if they are to swamp or obliterate the characters of species; but, as all hybrids tend to break up when propagated by seeds, it must follow that bud-propagation would become more and more common, and this is associated in nature with decreased seed-production. Now, seed-production is the legitimate function of flowers; and we must concede that, as seed-production decreased, floriferousness must have decreased; and that, therefore, pronounced intercrossing would have obliterated the very organs upon which it depends, or have destroyed itself!

But I may be met by the objection that there is no inherent reason why hybrids should not become stable through seed-production by in-breeding, and I might be cited to the opinion of Darwin and others that in-breeding tends to fix any variety, whether it originates by crossing or other means. And it is a fact that in-breeding tends to fix varieties within certain limits, but those limits are often overpassed in the case of very pronounced crosses, whether cross-breeds or true hybrids. And if it is true, as all observation and experiments show, that sexual or reproductive powers of crosses are weakened as the cross becomes more violent, we should expect less and less possibility of successful in-breeding; for in-breeding without disastrous results is possible only with comparatively strong reproductive powers. As a matter of fact, it is found in practice that it is exceedingly difficult to fix pronounced hybrids by means of in-breeding. It sometimes happens, too, that the hybrid individual which we wish to perpetuate may be infertile with itself, as I have often found in the case of squashes. It is often advised that we cross the hybrid individual which we wish to fix with another like individual, or with one of its parents. These results are often successful, but oftener they are not. In the first place, it often happens that the hybrid individuals may be so diverse that no two of them are alike; this has been my experience in many crosses. And, again, crossing with a parent may draw the hybrid back again to the parental form. So long ago as last century Kölreuter proved this fact upon nicotiana and dianthus. A hybrid between Nicotiana rustica and N. paniculata was crossed with N. paniculata until it was indistinguishable from it; and it was then crossed with N. rustica until it became indistinguishable from that parent. Yet there is no other way of fixing a hybrid to be propagated by seeds than by in-breeding, and by constant attention to selection. Fortunately, it occasionally happens that a hybrid is stable, and therefore needs no fixing.

In this connection I may cite some of my own experience in crossing egg-plants and squashes; for, although the products were not true hybrids in the strict interpretation of the word, many of them were hybrids to all intents and purposes, because made between very unlike varieties, and they will serve to illustrate the difficulties of which I speak. Offspring of egg-plant crosses were grown in 1890, and upon some of the most promising plants some flowers were self-pollinated. But these self-pollinated seeds gave just as variable offspring in 1891, as those selected almost at random from the patch; and, what was worse, none of them reproduced the parent, or " came true to seed," and all further motive for in-breeding was gone. My labor, therefore, amounted to nothing more than my own edification. My experience in crossing pumpkins and squashes has now extended through many years; and, although I have obtained about one thousand types not named or described, I have not yet succeeded in fixing one. The difficulty here is an aggravated one, however. The species are so exceedingly variable that all the hybrid individuals may be unlike, so that there can be no crossing between identical stocks; and, if in-breeding is attempted, it may be found that the flowers will not in-breed. And the refusal to in-breed is all the more strange because the sexes are separated in different flowers upon the same plant. In other words, in my experience, it is very difficult to get good seeds from squashes which are fertilized by a flower upon the same vine. The squashes may grow normally to full maturity, but be entirely hollow, or contain only empty seeds. In some instances the seeds may appear to be good, but may refuse to grow under the best conditions. Finally, a small number of flowers may give good seeds. I have many times observed this refusal of squashes (Cucurbita Pepo) to in-breed. It was first brought to my attention through efforts to fix certain types into varieties. The figures of one season's tests will sufficiently indicate the character of the problem. In 1890, one hundred and eighty-five squash flowers were carefully pollinated with staminate flowers taken from the same vine which bore the pistillate flowers. Only twenty-two of these produced fruit, and of these only seven, or less than one-third, bore good seeds, and in some of these the seeds were few. Now, these twenty-two fruits represented as many different varieties, so that the inability to set fruit with pollen from the same vine is not a peculiarity of a particular variety. The records of the seeds of the seven fruits in 1891 are as follows : —

Fruit No. 1. — Four vines were obtained, with four different types, two of them being white, one yellow, and one black.

Fruit No. 2. — Twenty-three vines. Fifteen types very unlike, twelve being white and three yellow.

Fruit No. 3. — Two vines. One type of fruit which was almost like one of the original parents.

Fruit No. 4. — Thirty-two vines. Six types, differing chiefly in size and shape.

Fruit No. 5. — Twenty vines. Nineteen types, of which ten were white, eight orange, one striped, and all very unlike.

Fruit No. 6. — Thirteen vines. Eleven types, — eight yellow, two black, one white.

Fruit No. 7. — One vine.

These offspring were just as variable as those from flowers not in-bred, and no more likely, apparently, to reproduce the parent. These tests leave me without any method of fixing a pronounced cross of squashes, and lead me to think that the legitimate process of origination of new kinds here, as, indeed, if not in general, is a more gradual process of selection, coupled, perhaps, with minor crossing.

I will relate a definite attempt towards the fixation of a squash which I had obtained from crossing. The history of it runs back to 1887, when a cross was effected between a summer yellow crookneck and a white bush scallop squash. In 1889 there appeared a squash of great excellence, combining the merits of summer and winter squashes with very attractive form, size, and color, and a good habit of plant. I showed the fruit to one of the most expert seedsmen of the country, and he pronounced it one of the most promising types which he had ever seen; and, as he informed me that he had fixed squashes by breeding in and in, I was all the more anxious to carry out my own convictions in the same direction. It is needless to say that I was very happy over what I regarded as a great triumph. Of course I must have a large number of plants of my new variety, that I might select the best, both for in-breeding and for crossing similar types. So I selected the very finest squash, having placed it where I could admire it for some days, and saved every seed of it. These seeds were planted upon the most conspicuous knoll in my garden in 1890. It was soon evident that something was wrong. I seemed to have everything except my squash. One plant, however, bore fruits almost like the parent, and upon this I began my attempts towards in-breeding. But flower after flower failed, and I soon saw that the plant was infertile with itself. Careful search revealed two or three other plants very like this one, and I then proceeded to make crosses upon it. I was equally confident that this method would succeed. When I harvested my squashes in the fall and took account of stock, I found that the seeds of my one squash had given just as many different types as there were plants, and I actually counted one hundred and ten kinds distinct enough to be named and recognized. Still confident, in 1891 I planted the seeds of my few crosses, and as the summer days grew long and the crickets chirped in the meadows, I watched the expanding squash blossoms and wondered what they would bring forth. But they brought only disappointment. Not one seed produced a squash like the parent. My squash had taken an unscientific leave of absence, and I do not know its whereabouts. And when the frost came and killed every ambitious blossom, my hope went out and has not yet returned!

Let us now recall how many undoubted hybrids there are, named and known, among our fruits and vegetables. In grapes there are the most. There are Rogers' hybrids, like the Agawam, Lindley, Wilder, Salem, and Barry; and there is some reason for supposing that the Delaware, Catawba, and other varieties are of hybrid origin. And many hybrids have come to notice lately through the work of Munson and others. But it must be remembered that grapes are naturally exceedingly variable, and the specific limits are not well known, and that hybridization among them lacks much of that definiteness which ordinarily attaches to the subject. In pears there is the Kieffer class. In apples, peaches, plums, cherries, gooseberries, and currants, there are no important commercial hybrids. In blackberries there is the blackberry-dewberry class, represented by the Wilson Early and others. Some of the raspberries, like the Philadelphia and Shaffer, are hybrids between the red and black species. Hybrids have been produced between the raspberry and blackberry by two or three persons, but they possess no promise of economic results. Among all the list of garden vegetables (plants which are propagated by seeds) I do not know of a single important hybrid; and the same is true of wheat, — unless the Carman wheat-rye varieties become prominent, — oats, the grasses, and other farm crops. But among ornamental plants there are many; and it is a significant fact that the most numerous, most marked, and most successful hybrids occur in the plants most carefully cultivated and protected, those, in other words, which are farthest removed from all untoward circumstances and an independent position. This is nowhere so well illustrated as in the case of cultivated orchids, in which hybridization has played no end of freaks, and in which, also, every individual plant is nursed and coddled.[1] With such plants the struggle for existence is reduced to its lowest terms; for it must be borne in mind that, even in the garden, plants must fight severely for a chance to live, and even then only the very best can persist, or are even allowed to try.

I am sure that this list of hybrids is much more meagre than most catalogues and trade-lists would have us believe, but I am sure that it is approximately near the truth. It is, of course, equivalent to saying that most of the so-called hybrid fruits and vegetables are myths. There is everywhere a misconception of what a hybrid is, and how it comes to exist; and yet, perhaps because of this indefinite knowledge, there is a wide-spread feeling that a hybrid is necessarily good, while the presumption is directly the opposite. The identity of a hybrid in the popular mind rests entirely upon some superficial character, and proceeds upon the assumption that it is necessarily intermediate between the parents. Hence we find one of our popular authors asserting that, because the kohlrabi bears its thickened portion midway of its stem, it is evidently a hybrid between the cabbage and turnip, which bear respectively the thickened parts

[1] Consult E. Bohnhof, "Dictionnaire des Orchidées Hybrides," Paris, 1895.

at the opposite extremities of the stem! And then there are those who confound the word hybrid with *high-bred*, and who build attractive castles upon the unconscious error. And thus is confusion confounded!

But, before leaving this subject of hybridization, I must speak of the old yet common notion that there is some peculiar influence exerted by each sex in the parentage of hybrids; for I shall thereby not only call your attention to what I believe to be an error, but shall also find the opportunity to still further illustrate the entanglements of hybridization. It was held by certain early observers, of whom the great Linnæus was one, that the female parent determines the constitution of the hybrid, while the male parent gives the external attributes, as form, size, and color. The accumulated experience of nearly a century and a half appears to contradict this proposition, and Focke, who has recently gone over the whole ground, positively declares that it is untrue. There are instances, to be sure, in which this old idea is affirmed, but there are others in which it is contradicted. The truth appears to be this, — that the parent of greater strength or virility makes the stronger impression upon the hybrids, whether it is the staminate or pistillate parent; and it appears to be equally true that it is usually impossible to determine beforehand which parent is the stronger. It is certain that strength does not lie in size, neither in the high development of any character. It appears to be more particularly associated with what we call fixity or stability of character, or the tendency towards invariability.

This has been well illustrated in my own experiments with squashes, gourds, and pumpkins. The common little pear-shaped gourd will impress itself more strongly upon crosses than any of the edible squashes and pumpkins with which it will effect a cross, whether it is used as male or female parent. Even the imposing and ubiquitous great field pumpkin, which every New Englander associates with pies, is overpowered by the little gourd. Seeds from a large and sleek pumpkin which had been fertilized by gourd pollen, produced gourds and small hard-shelled globular fruits which were entirely inedible. A more interesting experiment was made between the handsome green-striped Bergen fall squash and the little pear gourd. Several flowers of the gourd were pollinated by the Bergen in 1889. The fruits raised from these seeds in 1890 were remarkably gourd-like. Some of these crosses were pollinated again in 1890 by the Bergen, and the seeds were sown in 1891. Here, then, were crosses into which the gourd had gone once and the Bergen twice, and both the parents are to all appearances equally fixed, the difference in strength, if any, attaching rather to the Bergen.

Now, the crop of 1891 still carried pronounced characters of the gourd. Even in the fruits which most resembled the Bergen, the shells were almost flinty hard, and the flesh, even when thick and tender, was bitter. Some of the fruits looked so much like the Bergen that I was led to think that the gourd had largely disappeared. The very hard but thin paper-like shell which the gourd had laid over the thick yellow flesh of the Bergen, I thought might serve a useful purpose, and make the squash a better keeper. And I found that it was a great protection, for the squash could stand any amount of rough handling, and was even not injured by ten degrees of frost. All this was an acquisition, and, as the squash was handsome and exceedingly productive, nothing more seemed to be desired. But it still remained to have a squash for dinner. The cook complained of the hard shell, but, once inside, the flesh was thick and attractive, and it cooked nicely. But the flavor! Dregs of quinine, gall, and boneset! The gourd was still there!

VI. UNCERTAINTIES OF POLLINATION.

We have now seen that uncertainty follows hybridization, and, in closing, I will say that uncertainty also attaches to the mere act of pollination. Between some species which are closely allied and which have large and strong flowers, four-fifths of the attempts towards cross-pollination may be successful; but such a large proportion of successes is not common, and it may be infrequent even in pollinations between plants of the same species or variety. Some of the failure is due in many cases to unskilful operation, but even the most expert operators fail as often as they succeed in promiscuous pollinating. There is good reason to believe, as Darwin has shown, that the failure may be due to some selective power of individual plants, by which they refuse pollen which is, in many instances, acceptable to other plants even of the same variety or stock. The lesson to be drawn from these facts is that operations should be as many as possible, and that discouragement should not come from failure. In order to illustrate the varying fortunes of the pollinator, I will transcribe some notes from my field-book.

Two hundred and thirty-four pollinations of gourds, pumpkins, and squashes, mostly between varieties of one species (Cucurbita Pepo), and including some individual pollinations, gave one hundred and seventeen failures and one hundred and seventeen successes. These crosses were made in varying weather, from July 28 to August 30. In some periods nearly all the operations would succeed, and at other times most of them would fail. I have always regarded these experiments as among my most successful ones, and yet but half of the pollinations "took." But one must not understand that I actually secured seeds from even all these one hundred and seventeen fruits, for some of them turned out to be seedless, and some were destroyed by insects before they were ripe, or they were lost by accidental means. A few more than half of the successful pollinations — if by success we mean the formation and growth of fruit — really secured us seeds, or about one-fourth of the whole number of efforts.

Twenty pollinations were made between potato flowers, and they all failed; also, seven pollinations of red peppers, four of husk-tomato, two of Nicotiana affinis upon petunia and two of the reciprocal cross, twelve of radish, one of Mirabilis Jalapa upon M. longiflora and two of the reciprocal cross, three Convolvulus major upon C. minor and one of the reciprocal, one muskmelon by squash, two muskmelons by watermelon, and one muskmelon by cucumber.

This is but one record. Let me give another: —

Cucumber, ninety-five efforts: fifty-two successes, forty-three failures. Tomato, forty-three efforts: nineteen successes, twenty-four failures. Egg-plant, seven efforts: one success, six failures. Pepper, fifteen efforts: one success, fourteen failures. Husk-tomato, forty-five efforts: forty-five failures. Pepino, twelve efforts: twelve failures. Petunia by Nicotiana affinis, eleven efforts: eleven failures. Nicotiana affinis by petunia, six efforts: six failures. General Grant tobacco by Nicotiana affinis, eleven efforts: eight successes, three failures. Nicotiana affinis by General Grant tobacco, fifteen efforts: fifteen failures. General Grant tobacco by General Grant tobacco, one effort: one success. Nicotiana affinis by Nicotiana affinis, three efforts: two successes, one failure. Tuberous begonia, five efforts: five successes.

Total, three hundred and twelve efforts: eighty-nine successes, two hundred and twenty-three failures.

Conclusion.

And now, the sum of it all is this: encourage in every way crosses within the limits of the variety and in connection with change of stock, expecting increase in vigor and productiveness; hybridize if you wish to experiment, but do it carefully, systematically, thoroughly, and do not expect too much. Extend Darwin's famous proposition to read: Nature abhors both perpetual self-fertilization and hybridization.

LECTURE III.

HOW DOMESTIC VARIETIES ORIGINATE.

"The key is man's power of accumulative selection: nature gives successive variations; man adds them up in certain directions useful to him." This, in Darwin's phrase, is the essence of the cultivator's skill in ameliorating the vegetable kingdom. So far as man is concerned, the origin of the initial variation is largely chance, but this start or variation once given, he has the power, in most cases, to perpetuate it and to modify its characters. There are, then, two very different factors or problems in the origination of garden varieties,—the production of the first departure or variation, and the subsequent breeding of it. Persons who give little thought to the subject, look upon variation as the end of their endeavors, thinking that a form comes into being with all its characters well marked and fixed. In reality, however, variation is but the beginning; selection is the end.

I. INDETERMINATE VARIETIES.

There are two general classes of garden varieties as respects the method of their origin,—

those which come into existence somewhat suddenly and which require little else of the husbandman than the multiplication of them, and those which are the result of a slow evolution or direct breeding. The former are indeterminate or uncertain, and the latter are determinate or definite. The greater part of those in the first class are plants which are multiplied or divided by bud-propagation. They comprise nearly all our fruits, the woody ornamental plants, and such herbaceous genera as begonia, canna, gladiolus, lily, dahlia, carnation, chrysanthemum, and the like,— in fact, all those multiplied by grafting, cuttings, bulbs, or other asexual parts. The original plant may be either a seedling or a bud-sport. The gardener, who is always on the lookout for novelties, discovers its good qualities and propagates it.

Varieties which are habitually multiplied by buds, as in those plants which I have mentioned in the last paragraph, vary widely when grown from seeds, so that every seedling may be markedly distinct. As soon, however, as varieties are widely and exclusively propagated by seeds, they develop a capacity of carrying the greater part of the individual differences down to the offspring. That is, seedlings from bud-multiplied plants do not "come true," as a rule, whilst those from seed-propagated plants do "come true." The reason of this difference will become apparent upon a moment's reflection. In the seed-propagated plants, like the kitchen-garden vegetables and the annual flowers, we select the seeds and thereby eliminate all those variations which would have arisen had the discarded seeds been sown. In other words, we are constantly fixing the tendency to "come true," for this feature of plants is as much a variation as form or color or any other attribute is. Suppose, for instance, that a certain variation were to receive two opposite treatments, the seeds from one-half of the progeny being carefully selected year by year, and all those from untypical plants discarded, whilst in the other half all the seeds from all the plants, whether good or bad, are saved and sown. In the one case, it will be seen, we are fixing the tendency to "come true," for this is all that constitutes a horticultural variety,— a brood which is very much like all its parents. In the other case, we are constantly eliminating the tendency to "come true" by allowing every modifying agency full sway. So the very act of taking seeds only from plants which have "come true," tends to still more strongly fix the hereditary force within narrow limits. Working against this restrictive force, however, are all the agencies of environment, so that, fortunately, now and then a seed gives a "rogue," or a plant widely unlike its parent, and this may be the start for a new variety.

With bud-multiplied varieties, however, the case is very different. Here every seed may be sown, as in the illustrative case above, because the seedlings are not wanted for themselves, but simply as stocks upon which to bud or graft the desired varieties. So there is no seed selection in the ordinary propagation of apples, pears, peaches, and the other orchard fruits. The seeds are taken indiscriminately from pomace or the refuse of canning and evaporating factories. But every annual garden vegetable is always grown from seeds more or less carefully saved from plants which possess some desired attribute. There is no reason why the tree fruits should not reproduce themselves from seeds just as closely as the annual herbs do, if they were to be as carefully propagated by selected seeds through a long course of generations. There is excellent proof of this in the well-marked races or families of Russian apples. In that country, grafting has been little employed, and consequently it has been necessary to select seeds only from acceptable trees in order that the offspring might be more acceptable. So the Russian apples have come to run in groups or families, each family bearing the mark of some strong ancestor. Most of the seedlings of the Duchess of Oldenburg are recognizable because of their likeness to the parent. We may thus trace an incipient tendency in our own fruits towards racial characters. The Fameuse type of apples, for example, tends to perpetuate itself ; and a similar tendency is very well marked in the Damson and Green Gage plums, the Orange quince, Concord grape, and Hill's Chili and Crawford peaches. But inasmuch as bud-multiplication is so essential in nursery practice, we can hardly hope for the time when our trees and shrubs, or even our perennial herbs, will "come true" with much certainty. In them, therefore, we get new varieties by simply sowing the seeds; but in seed-propagated varieties we must depend either upon chance variations or else we must resort to definite plant-breeding.

II. Plant-breeding.

The breeding of domestic animals is attended, for the most part, with such definite and often precise results that there has come to be a general desire to extend the same principles to plants. It is not unusual to hear well-informed people say that it is possible to breed plants with as much certainty and exactness as it is to breed animals. The fact is, however, that such exactness will never be possible, because plants are very unlike animals in organization, and because, also, the objects sought in the two cases are fundamentally unlike. Plants, as we have seen, are made up of a colony of potential individuals, and to breed between two plants by crossing means that we must choose the sex-parents from amongst as many individuals as there are flowers or branches on the two plants, whilst in animals we choose two definite personal parents. And these personal parents are either male or female, and the union is essential to the production of offspring, whilst in plants each parent — that is, each flower — is generally both male and female, and the union of two is not essential to the production of offspring, for the plant is capable of multiplying itself by buds. The element of chance, therefore, is one hundred, or more, to one in crossing plants as compared with crossing animals. Then, again, the plant-parents are modified profoundly by every environmental condition of soil and temperature and sunshine, or other external condition, since they possess no bodily temperature, no choice of conditions, and no volition to enable them to overcome the circumstances in which they are placed. Animals, on the contrary, have all these elements of personality, and the breeder is also able to control the conditions of their lives to a nicety. In view of all these facts, it is not strange that animals can be bred by crossing with more confidence than plants can. But there is another and even more important difference between the breeding of animals and the breeding of plants. In animals, our sole object is to secure simply one animal or one brood of offspring. In plants, our object is, in general, to secure a race or generations of offspring, which may be disseminated freely over the earth. In the bovine race, for example, our object in breeding is to produce one cow with given characters; in turnips, our object is to produce a new variety, the seed of which will reproduce the variety, whether sown in Pennsylvania or Ceylon. It is apparent, therefore, that any comparisons drawn between the breeding of animals and plants are fundamentally fallacious.

Is there, then, any such thing as plant-breeding, any possibility that the operator can proceed with some confidence that he may obtain the ideal which he has in mind? Yes, to a certain extent.

It is apparent that the very first effort on the part of the plant-breeder must be to secure individual differences; for so long as the plants which he handles are very closely alike, so long there will be little hope of obtaining new varieties. He must, therefore, cause his plants to vary. In plants which are comparatively unvariable, it is frequently impossible to produce variations in the desired direction at once, but it is more important to "break" the type,—that is, to make it depart markedly from its normal behavior in any or many directions (page 19). If the type once begins to vary, to break up into different forms, the operator may be sure that it will soon become plastic enough to allow of modification in the manner which he desires. But whilst it is important or even necessary to break a well-marked type into many forms, it would no doubt be unwise to encourage this tendency after it once appears, lest the plant acquire a too strong habit of scattering. This initial variation is induced by changing the conditions in which the plant has habitually grown, as a change of seed, change of soil, tillage, varying the food supply, crossing, and the like.

As a matter of fact, however, nearly all plants which have been long cultivated are already sufficiently variable to afford a starting-point for breeding. The operator should have a vivid mental picture of the variety which he designs to obtain; then he should select that plant in his plantation which is the nearest his ideal, and sow the seeds of it. From the seedlings he should again select the individuals which most nearly approach his type, and so on, generation after generation, until the desired object is attained. It is important, if he is to make rapid progress, that he keep the same ideal in mind year by year, otherwise there will be vacillation and the progress of one year may be undone by a counter movement the following year. In this way, it will be found that almost any character of a plant may be either intensified or lessened. This is man's nearest approach to the Creator in his dominion over the physical forms of life, and it is great and potent in proportion as it sets for itself correct ideals in the beginning and adheres to them until the end.

When beginning this selection or breeding for an ideal, it is important that impossible or contradictory results should be avoided. Some of the cautions and suggestions which need to be considered are these: —

1. *Avoid striving after features which are antagonistic or foreign to the species or genus with which you are working.* Every group of plants has become endowed with certain characters or lines of development, and the cultivator will secure quicker and surer results if he works along the same lines, rather than to attempt to thwart them. Nature gives the hint: let men follow it out, rather than to endeavor to create new types of characters. Let us take some of the solanaceous plants as examples. There are certain types of the genus solanum which have a natural habit of tuber-bearing, as the potato. Such species should be bred for tubers and not for fruits. There are other solanums, however, like the egg-plants and the pepinoes, which naturally vary or develop in

the direction of fruit-bearing, and these should be bred for fruits and not for tubers; and the same should be true in the related genera of tomatoes, red peppers, and physalis. Those ambitious persons who are always looking for a tuber-bearing tomato, therefore, might better concentrate their energies on the potato, for the tomato is not developing in that direction; and even if the tomato could be made to produce tubers, it would thereby lessen its fruit production, for plants cannot maintain two diverse and profitable crops at the same time. It is more reasonable, and certainly more practicable, to grow potatoes on potato plants and tomatoes on tomato plants.

2. *The quickest and most marked results are to be expected in those groups or species which are normally the most variable.* There are a greater number of variations or starting-points in such species; but it also follows that the forms are less stable the more the species is variable. Yet the variations, being very plastic, yield themselves readily to the wishes of the operator. Carrière puts the thought in this form: "The stability of forms, in any group of plants, is, in general, in inverse ratio to the number of the species which it contains, and also to the degree of its domestication."

The most variable types are the most dominant ones over the earth; that is, they occur in greater numbers and under more diverse conditions than the comparatively invariable types do. The compositæ, or sunflower-like plants, comprise a ninth or tenth of the total species of flowering plants, and the larger part of the subordinate types or genera contain many forms or species. Aster, goldenrod, the hawkweeds, thistles, and other groups, are representative of the cosmopolitan or variable types of composites. Whenever, for any reason, any type begins to decline in variability, it also begins to perish; it is then tending towards extinction. Monotypic genera—those which contain but a single species—are generally of local or disconnected distribution, and are, for the most part, vanishing remnants of a once dominant or important type. As a rule, most of our widely variable and staple cultivated species are members of large, or at least polytypic genera. Such, for example, are the apples and pears, peaches and plums, oranges and lemons, roses, bananas, chrysanthemums, pinks, cucurbits, beans, potato, grapes, barley, rice, cotton. A marked exception to this statement is maize, which is immensely variable and is generally held to have come from a single species; but the genesis of maize is unknown, and it is possible, though scarcely probable, that more than one species is concerned in it. Wheat is also a partial exception, although the original specific type is not understood; and the latest monographers admit three or four other species to the genus, aside from wheat. There are other exceptions, but they are mostly unimportant, and, in the main, it may be said that the dominant domestic types of plants represent markedly polytypic genera.

3. *Breed for one thing at a time.* The person who strives at the same time for increase or modification in prolificacy and flavor will be likely to fail in both. He should work for one object alone, simply giving sufficient attention to subsidiary objects to keep them up to normal standard. This is really equivalent to saying that there can be no such thing as the perfect all-around variety which so many people covet. Varieties must be adapted to specific uses, — one for shipping, one for canning, one for dessert, one for keeping qualities, and the like. The more good varieties there are of any species, the more widely and successfully that species can be cultivated.

4. *Do not desire contradictory attributes in any variety.* A variety, for example, which bears the maximum number of fruits or flowers cannot be expected to greatly increase the size of those organs without loss in numbers. This is well shown in the tomato. The original tomato produced from six to ten fruits in a cluster, but as the fruits increased in size the numbers in each cluster fell to two or three. That is, increase in size proceeded somewhat at the expense of numer-

ical productivity; yet the total weight of fruit per plant has greatly increased. The same is true of apples and pears; for whilst these trees bear flowers in clusters, they generally bear their fruits singly. Originally, every flower normally set fruit. The reason why blackberries, currants, and grapes do not increase more markedly in size, is probably because the size of cluster has been given greater attention than the size of berry. Plants which now bear a full crop of tubers cannot be expected to increase greatly in fruit-bearing, as I have already explained under Rule 1. This fact is illustrated in the potato, in which, as tuber production has increased, seed production has decreased, so that potato growers now complain that potatoes do not produce bolls as freely as they did years ago.

5. *When selecting seeds, remember that the character of the whole plant is more important than the character of any one branch or part of the plant; and the more uniform the plant in all its parts, the greater is the likelihood that it will transmit its characters.* If one is striving for larger flowers, for instance, he will secure better results if he choose seeds from plants which bear large flowers throughout, than he will if he choose them from some one large-flowering branch on a plant which bears indifferent flowers on the remaining branches, even though this given branch produce much larger

flowers than those borne on the large-flowered plant. Small potatoes from productive hills give a better product than large potatoes from unproductive hills. The practice of selecting large ears from a bin of corn, or large melons from the grocer's wagon, is much less efficient in producing large products the following season than the practice of going into the fields and selecting the most uniformly large-fruited parents would be. A very poor plant may occasionally produce one or two very superior fruits, but the seeds are more likely to perpetuate the characters of the plant than of the fruits.

The following experiences detailed by Henri L. de Vilmorin illustrate my proposition admirably: "I tried an experiment with seeds of Chrysanthemum carinatum gathered on double, single, and semi-double heads, all growing on one plant, and found no difference whatever in the proportion of single and double-flowered plants. In striped verbenas, an unequal distribution of the color is often noticed; some heads are pure white, some of a self color, and most are marked with colored stripes on white ground. I had seeds taken severally from all and tested alongside one another. The result was the same. All the seeds from one plant, whatever the color of the flower that bore them, gave the same proportion of plain and variegated flowers."

UNIFORMNESS IN THE PARTS. 101

The second part of my proposition is equally as important as the first,—the fact that a plant which is uniform in all its branches or parts is more likely to transmit its general features than one which varies within itself. It is well known that bean plants often produce beans with various styles of markings on the same plant or even in the same pod, yet these variations rarely ever perpetuate themselves. The same remark may be applied to variations in peas. These illustrations only add emphasis to the fact that intending plant-breeders should give greater heed than they usually do to the entire plant, rather than confine their attention to the particular part or organ which they desire to improve.

At first thought, it may look as if these facts are directly opposed to the proposition which I emphasized in my first lecture, that every branch of a plant is a potential autonomy, but it is really a confirmation of it. The variation itself shows that the branch is measurably independent, but it is not until the conditions or causes of the variation are powerful enough to affect the entire plant that they are sufficiently impressed upon the organization of the plant to make their effects hereditary.

There is an apparent exception to the law that the character of the entire plant is more important than any one organ or part of it, in the case of the seeds themselves. That is, better results usually follow the sowing of large and heavy seeds than of small or unselected seeds from the same plant. This, however, does not affect the main proposition, for the seed is in a measure independent of the plant-body, and is not so directly influenced by environment as the other organs are. And, again, the seed receives a part of its elements from a second or male parent. The good results which follow the use of large seeds are, chiefly, greater uniformity of crop, increased vigor, often a gain in earliness and sometimes in bulk, and generally a greater capacity for the production of seeds. These results are probably associated less with any innate hereditable tendencies than with the mere vegetative strength and uniformness of the large seeds. The large seeds usually germinate more quickly than the small ones, provided both are equally mature, and they push the plantlet on more vigorously. This initial gain, coming at the most critical time in the life of the new individual, is no doubt responsible for very much of the result which follows. The uniformity of crop is the most important advantage which comes of the use of large seeds, and this is obviously the result of the elimination of all seeds of varying degrees of maturity, of incomplete growth and formation, and of low vitality.

Another important consideration touching the selection of seeds is the fact that very immature seeds give a feeble but precocious progeny. This has long been observed by gardeners, but Sturtevant, Arthur, and Goff have recently made a critical examination of the subject. "It is not the slightly unripe seeds that give a noticeable increase in earliness," according to Arthur, "but very unripe seeds, gathered from fruit [tomatoes] scarcely of full size and still very green. Such seeds do not weigh more than two-thirds as much as those fully ripe. They germinate readily, but the plantlets lack constitutional vigor and are more easily affected by retarding or harmful influences. If they can be brought through the early period of growth and become well established, and the foliage or fruit is not attacked by rots or blights, the grower will usually be rewarded by an earlier and more abundant crop of slightly smaller and less firm fruit. These characters will be more strongly emphasized in subsequent years by continuous seed propagation." Goff remarks that the increase in earliness in tomatoes, following the use of markedly immature seeds, "is accompanied by a marked decrease in the vigor of the plant, and in the size, firmness, and keeping quality of the fruit." These results are probably closely associated with the chemical constitution and content of the immature seeds.

The organic compounds have probably not yet reached a state of stability, and they therefore respond quickly to external stimuli when placed in conditions suitable to germination; and there is little food for the nourishment of the plantlet. The consequent weakness of the plantlet results in a loss of vegetative vigor, which is earliness (see Rule 11).

Still another feature connected with the choice of seeds is the fact that in some plants, as in some Ipomœas, for example, the color of the seed is more or less intimately associated with the color of the flower which produced them and also with the color of the flowers which they will produce.

6. *Plants which have any desired characteristics in common may differ widely in their ability to transmit these characters.* It is generally impossible for the cultivator to determine, from the appearance of any given number of similar plants, which of them will give progeny the most unvariable and the most like its parent; but it may be said that those individuals which grow in the most usual or normal environments are most likely to perpetuate themselves. A very unusual condition, as of soil, moisture, or exposure, is not easily imitated when providing for the succeeding generation, and a return to normal conditions of environment may be expected to be followed by a more or less complete return to normal attributes on the

part of the plant. If the same variation, therefore, were to occur in plants growing under widely different conditions, the operator who wishes to preserve the new form should take particular care to select his seeds from those individuals which seem to have been least influenced by the immediate conditions in which they have grown.

Again, if the same variation appears both in uncrossed and crossed plants, the best results should be expected in selecting seeds from the former. We have already seen, in the second lecture, how it is that crosses are unstable, and how the instability is apt to be the greater the more violent the cross. "Cross-breeding greatly increases the chance of wide variation," writes Henri L. de Vilmorin, "but it makes the task of fixation more difficult."

It is very important, therefore, when selecting seeds from plants which seem to give promise of a new variety, to sow the seeds of each plant separately, and then make the subsequent selections from the most stable generation; and it is equally important that the operator should not trust to a single plant as a starting-point, whenever he has several promising plants from which to choose.

7. *The less marked the departure from the genius of the normal type, the greater, in general, is the likelihood that it will be perpetuated.* That

is, widely aberrant forms are generally unstable. This is admirably illustrated in crosses. The seed-progeny of crosses between closely related varieties, or between different plants of the same variety, is more uniform and generally more easy of improvement by selection than the progeny of hybrids. In uncrossed plants, the general tendency is to resemble their parents, and the greater the number of like ancestors, the greater is the tendency to "come true." There is thought to be a tendency, though necessarily a weak one, to return to some particular ancestor, or to "date back." This is known as atavism. The so-called atavistic forms are likely to be unstable, to break up into numerous forms, or to return more or less completely to the type of the main line of the ancestry. The following statements touching some of the relations of atavism to the amelioration of plants, are the results of an excellent study of heredity in lupines by Louis Levêque de Vilmorin: —

"1. The tendency to resemble its parents is generally the strongest tendency in any plant;

"2. But it is notably impaired as it comes into conflict with the tendency to resemble the general line of its ancestry.

"3. This latter tendency, or atavism, is constant, though not strong, and scarcely becomes impaired by the intervention of a series of generations in which no reversion has taken place.

"4. The tendency to resemble a near progenitor (only two or three generations removed), on the other hand, is very soon obliterated if the given progenitor is different from the bulk of its ancestors."

8. *The crossing of plants should be looked upon as a means or starting-point, not as an end.* We cross two flowers and sow the seeds. The resulting seedlings may be unlike either parent. Here, then, is variation. The operator should select that plant which most nearly satisfies his ideal, and then, by selection from its progeny and the progeny of succeeding generations, gradually obtain the plant which he desires. It is only in plants which are propagated by asexual parts—as grafts, cuttings, layers, bulbs, and the like—that hybrids or crosses are commonly immediately valuable; for in these plants we really cut up and multiply the one individual plant which pleases us in the first batch of seedlings, rather than to take the offspring or seedlings of it. Thus, if any particular plant in a lot of seedlings of crosses of cannas, or plums, or hops, or strawberries, or potatoes, is valuable, we multiply that one individual. There is no occasion for fixing the variety. But any satisfactory plant in a lot of seedlings of crosses of pumpkins, or wheat, or beans, must be made the parent of a new variety by sowing the seeds of it and then by selecting for seed-

parents, year by year, those plants which are best. "The unsettled forms arising from crosses," Focke writes, "are the plastic material out of which gardeners form their varieties."

But even in the fruits, and other bud-propagated plants, crossing may often be used to as good advantage for the purpose of originating variation as it can in peas or buckwheat. It only requires a longer time to fix and select variations because the plants mature so slowly. Ordinarily, if the operator does not find satisfactory plants amongst the seedlings of any cross of fruit trees, he roots up the whole batch as profitless. But if he were to allow the best plants to stand and were to sow seeds from them, the second generation might produce something more to his liking. But it is generally quicker to make another cross and to try the experiment over again, than to wait for unpromising seedlings to bear. This repeated repetition of the experiment, however, — continual crossing and sowing and uprooting, — is gambling. Throwing dice to see what will turn up is a comparable proceeding. The sowing of uncrossed seed is little better. Peter M. Gideon sowed over a bushel of apple seed, and one seed produced the Wealthy apple.[1]

---

[1] The facts in the origination of the Wealthy apple, as related to me by Mr. Gideon, are these: he first planted a bushel of apple seeds, and then each year, for nine years, he planted

D. B. Wier raised a million seedlings of soft maple, and one plant of the lot had finely divided leaves, and is now Wier's Cutleaved maple. Teas' Weeping mulberry, which is now so deservedly popular, was, as Mr. Teas tells me, "merely an accidental seedling." So this explains why the production of new varieties of fruits is always chance, whilst a skilled man can sit in his study in the winter time and picture to himself a new bean or muskmelon, and then go out in the next three or four summers and produce it.

9. *If it is desired to employ crossing as a direct means of producing new varieties, each parent to the proposed cross should be selected in agreement with the rules already specified, and also because it possesses in an emphatic degree one or more of the qualities which it is desired to combine; and the more uniformly and persistently the parent presents a given character, the greater is the chance that it will transmit that character.* It has already been said that crossing for the instant production of new varieties is most certain to give valuable

enough seed to give a thousand trees. At the end of ten years, all the seedlings had perished (this was in Minnesota) except one hardy seedling crab. Then a small lot of seeds of apples and crab apples was obtained in Maine, and from these the Wealthy came. There were only about fifty seeds in the batch of crab seed which gave the Wealthy; but before this variety was obtained, much over a bushel of seed had been sown.

results in those species which are propagated by buds, because the initial individual differences are not dissipated by seed-reproduction. This is especially true of hybridization, or crossing between distinct species; for in such violent crossing as this the offspring is particularly likely to be unstable when propagated by seeds. The results of hybridization appear to be most certain in those plants which are grown under glass, and in which, therefore, the selection of the seed-parents is most carefully made, and where the conditions of existence are most uniform. The most remarkable results in hybridization which have yet been attained are with the choicer glasshouse plants, such as orchids, begonias, anthuriums, and the like. (Lecture II.)

The more violent the cross, the less is the likelihood that desirable offspring will follow. Species which refuse to give satisfactory results when hybridized directly or between the pure stocks, may give good varieties when the "blood" has become somewhat attenuated through previous crossings. The best results in hybridizing our native grape with the European grape, for example, have come from the use of one parent which is already a hybrid. Two notable examples are the Brighton and Diamond grapes, raised by Jacob Moore. The Brighton is a cross of Concord (pure native) by Diana-Hamburg (hybrid of impure native and European). Diamond is a cross of Concord by Iona, the latter parent undoubtedly of impure origin, containing a trace of the European vine. T. V. Munson's Brilliant is a secondary hybrid, its parents, Lindley and Delaware, both containing hybrid blood. Others of his varieties have similar histories. Even when the cross is much attenuated — or three or four or even more times removed from a pure hybrid origin by means of subsequent crossings — it may still produce marked effects in a cross without introducing such contradictory characters as to jeopardize the value of the offspring.

Amongst American fruit plants there are comparatively few valuable hybrids. The most conspicuous ones are in the grapes, particularly the various Rogers varieties, such as Agawam, Lindley, Wilder, Barry, and others, which are hybrids of the European grape and a native species. Other hybrids are the Kieffer and allied pears (between the common pear and the Oriental pear), the Transcendent and a few other crabs (between the common apple and the Siberian crab), the Soulard and kindred crabs (between the common apple and the native Western crab), a few blackberries of the Wilson Early type (between the blackberry and the dewberry), the purple-cane raspberries (between the native red and black raspberries, and possibly sometimes combined with the European raspberry), the Utah Hybrid cherry (between the Western sand cherry and the sand plum), and probably a few of the native plums. There is undoubtedly a fertile field for further work in hybridizing our fruits, particularly those of native origin, and also many of the ornamental plants; the danger is that persons are apt to expect too much from hybridization, and too little from the betterment of all the other conditions which so profoundly modify plants. Violent hybridizations generally give unsatisfactory and unreliable results; but subsequent crossings, when the "blood" of the original species to the contract is considerably attenuated, may be expected to correct or overcome the first incompatibility, as explained above.

10. *Establish the ideal of the desired variety firmly in the mind before any attempt is made at plant-breeding.* If one is to make any progress in securing new varieties, he must first be an expert judge of the capabilities and merits of the plants with which he is dealing, otherwise he may attempt the impossible or he may obtain a variety which has no merit. It is important, too, that the person bear in mind the fact that a variety which is simply as good as any other in cultivation is not worth introducing. It should be better in some particular than any other in existence. The operator must know the

points of his plant, as an expert stock-breeder knows the points of an animal, and he must possess the rare judgment to determine which characters are most likely to reappear in the offspring. Inasmuch as a person can be an expert in only a few plants, it follows that he cannot expect satisfactory results in breeding any species which may chance to come before him. Persistent and uniform effort, continued over a series of years, is generally demanded for the production of really valuable varieties. Thus it often happens that one man excels all competitors in breeding a particular class of plants. The horticulturist will recall, for instance, Lemoine in the breeding of gladiolus, Eckford in peas, Crozy in cannas, Bruant in pelargoniums, and others. There are now and then varieties which arise from no effort, but because of that very fact they reflect no credit upon the so-called originator, who is really only the lucky finder. So far as the originator is concerned, such varieties are merely chance. If, however, the operator — himself an expert judge of the plant with which he deals — chooses his seeds with care and discrimination, and then proposes, if need be, to follow up his work generation by generation by means of selection, the work becomes plant-breeding of the highest type.

First of all, therefore, the operator must know

what he can likely get, and what will likely be worth getting. Most persons, however, begin at the other end of the problem, — they get what they can, and then let the public judge if the effort has been worth the while.

11. *Having obtained a specific and correct ideal, the operator must next seek to make his plant vary in the desired direction.* This may be done by crossing, or by modifying the conditions under which the plant grows, as indicated in Lectures I. and II. If there are any two plants which possess indications of the desired attributes, cross them: amongst the seedlings there may be some which may serve as starting-points for further effort.

A change in the circumstances or environment of the plant may start the desired attribute. If the plant must be dwarfer, plant it on poorer or drier soil, transfer it towards the poles, plant it late in the season, or transplant it repeatedly (see pages 25 and 143). Dwarf peas become climbing peas on rich, moist soils. If the plant must have large fruits, allow it more food and room, and give attention to pruning and thinning. Certain geographical regions develop certain characters in plants, as we have seen (page 24); if, therefore, the desired feature does not appear spontaneously or as a result of any other treatment, transfer the plant for a time to that region which is characterized by such attributes, if there is any such.

The importance of growing the plant under conditions or environments in which the desired type of characters is most frequently found, is admirably emphasized in the evolution of varieties which are adapted to forcing under glass. Within a century,—and in many instances within a decade or two,—species which were practically unknown to glass-houses have produced varieties which are perfectly adapted to them. This has been accomplished by growing the most tractable existing varieties under glass, and then carefully and persistently selecting those which most completely adapt themselves to their environment and to the ideals of the operator. One of the most remarkable examples of this kind is afforded by the carnation. In Europe it is chiefly a border or out-door plant, but within a generation it has produced hosts of excellent forcing varieties in America, where it is grown almost exclusively as a glass-house flower. So the carnation types of Europe and America are widely unlike, and the unlikeness becomes more emphatic year by year because of the rapid aberrant evolution of the American forms.

Sowing the seeds of hardy annual plants in the fall often generates a tendency to produce thickened roots. The plant, finding itself unable to perfect seeds, stores its reserve in the root, and it therefore tends to become biennial. In this manner, with the aid of selection and the variation of the soil, Carrière was able to produce good radishes from the wild slender-rooted charlock (Raphanus Raphanistrum).

Lessened vigor, so long as the plant continues to be healthy, nearly always results in a comparative increase of fruits or reproductive organs. It is an old horticultural maxim that checking growth induces fruitfulness. It is largely in consequence of this fact that plants bear heaviest when they attain approximate maturity. Trees are often thrown into bearing by girdling, heavy pruning, the attacks of borers, and various accidental injuries. The gardener knows that if he keeps his plants in vigorous growth by constantly potting them on into larger pots, he will get little, or at least very late, bloom. The plant-breeder, therefore, may be able to induce the desired initial variation by attention to this principle. (See discussion of variation in relation to food supply, page 16.) Arthur has recently put the principle into this formula: "A decrease in nutrition during the period of growth of an organism, favors the development of the reproductive parts at the expense of the vegetative parts."

A most important means of inducing variation

is the simple change of seed, the philosophical reasons for which are explained on pages 59 and 28. A plant becomes closely fitted or accustomed to one set of conditions, and when it is placed in new conditions, it at once makes an effort to adapt itself to them. This adaptation is variation. No doubt the free interchange of seeds between seed-merchants and customers is one of the most fertile causes of the enormous increase in varieties in recent times.

When once a novel variety appears, others of a similar kind are likely soon to follow in other places, and some persons have supposed that there is a synchronistic variation in plants, or a tendency for like variations to appear simultaneously in widely separated localities. There is perhaps some remote reason for this belief, because there is, as Darwin expresses it, an accumulative effect of domestication or cultivation, by virtue of which plants which long remain comparatively invariable may within a short time, when cultivation has been continued long enough, vary widely and in many directions; and it is to be expected that even when plants have long since responded to the wishes of the cultivator, an equal amount or accumulation of the force of domestication would tend to produce like effects in different places. But it is probable that by far the greater part of this synchronistic variation is simply an apparent one, for whenever any marked novelty appears the attention of all interested persons is directed to looking for similar variations amongst their own plants.

12. *The person who is wishing for new varieties should look critically to all perennial plants, and particularly to trees and shrubs, for bud-varieties or sports.* It has already been said (pages 28, 6) that the branches of a tree may vary amongst themselves in the same way in which seedlings vary, and for the same reasons. As a rule, any marked sport is capable of being perpetuated by bud-propagation. The number of bud-varieties now in cultivation is really very large. Many of the cut-leaved and colored or variegated varieties of ornamental plants were originally found upon other trees as sports. The " mixing in the hill " of potatoes is bud-variation. Nectarines are derived from the peach, some of them as sports and some as seedlings. The moss-rose was probably originally a sport from the Provence rose. Greening apple trees often bear russet apples, and russet trees sometimes bear greenings. So far as I know, there are no varieties of annual plants which have originated as sports. The probable reason for this is the fact that the duration of the plant is short and that its constitution is not profoundly modified in a single generation by the new circumstances in which it is placed every

year. The effects of the conditions in which it lives are recorded in the seeds, and the plant dies without allowing a second season of growth to express the impressions which were received in a former generation. The fact that every branch of an annual plant — as of perennials — is unlike every other branch, is evidence enough that the annual is not unlike the perennial in fundamental constitution; and there is every reason to believe that if any given annual were to become a perennial, it would now and then develop differences sufficiently pronounced to make them worthy the name of sports, the same as hyacinths, bouvardias, trees, and all other perennial plants are apt to do.

Bud-varieties may not only come true from buds — as grafts, cuttings and layers, — but they occasionally perpetuate themselves by seeds. Now, these seedlings are amenable to selection, just the same as any other seedlings are; the bud-variety, therefore, may give the initial starting-point for plant-breeding. But, more than this, it is sometimes possible to improve and fix the type by bud-selection as well as by seed-selection. Darwin cites this interesting testimony: "Mr. Salter brings the principle of selection to bear on variegated plants propagated by buds, and has thus greatly improved and fixed several varieties. He informs me that at first a branch often produces variegated leaves on one side alone, and that the leaves are marked only with an irregular edging, or with a few lines of white and yellow. To improve and fix such varieties, he finds it necessary to encourage the buds at the bases of the most distinctly marked leaves and to propagate from them alone. By following, with perseverance, this plan during three or four successive seasons a distinct and fixed variety can generally be secured." Ernest Walker, a careful gardener at New Albany, Indiana, is of the opinion that the abnormal character of sports often intensifies itself if the sport is allowed to remain upon the parent plant for a considerable time. He has observed this particularly in coleus, where color sports are frequent. "In these," he says, "the sport begins with a branch, which may be taken off and propagated as a new variety. If left on the parent, other parts of the plant are apt to show similar variations. Indeed, I think it is not best to be in too great a hurry to remove a sporting branch, for its character seems to tend to become more fixed if it remains on the plant."

13. *The starting-point once given, all permanent progress lies in continued selection.* This, as I have already pointed out, is really the key to the whole matter. In the greater number of cases, the operator cannot produce the initial variation which he desires, but, by looking carefully amongst many plants, he may find one which shows an indication

of his ideal. This plant must be carefully saved, and all the seeds sown in a place where crossing with other types cannot take place. Of a hundred seedlings from this plant, mayhap one or two will still further emphasize the character which is sought. These, again, are saved and all the seeds are sown. So the operation goes on, patiently and persistently, and there is reward at the end. This is the one eternal and fundamental principle which underlies the amelioration of plants under the touch of man; and because we know, from experience, that it is so important, we are sure, as Darwin was, that selection in nature must be the most potent factor in the progress of the vegetable world.

But suppose this suggestion of the new variety does not appear amongst the batch of plants which we raise? Then sow again; vary the conditions; select the most widely variable types; cross; at length — if the ideal is true — the suggestion will come. "Cultivation, diversification of the conditions of existence, and repeated sowings" are the means which Verlot would employ to induce variations. But the skill and the character of the final result lie not so much in the securing of the initial start, as in the subsequent selection. Nature affords starting-points in endless number, but there are few men alert and skilful enough to take the hint and improve it. If I want a new tomato, I first endeavor to discover what I want. I decide that I must have one like the Acme in color, but more spherical, with a firmer flesh, and a little earlier. Then I shall raise an acre of Acme tomatoes, and closely allied varieties; or if I cannot do that, I make arrangements to inspect my neighbor's fields. I scrutinize every plant as the first fruits are ripening. Finally, I find one plant — not one fruit — which is something like the variety which I desire. Very well! Wait two to five years, and you shall see my new variety!

Some of these initial variations possess no tendency to reproduce themselves. The seedlings of them may break up into a great diversity of forms, no form representing the parent closely. In such cases, it is generally useless to proceed further with this brood. Another start should be made with another plant. So it is always important, as we have already seen (Rule 6), to have as many starting-points as possible, to lessen the risk of failure. Whilst it requires nice judgment to select those plants which possess the most important and the most transmissible combination of characters, the greatest skill is nevertheless required to carry forward a correct system of selection.

14. *Even when the desired variety is obtained, it must be kept up to the standard by constant attention to selection.* That is, there is no real stability in

the forms of plant life. So long as the conditions of existence vary, so long will plants make the effort to adapt themselves to the changes. No two seasons are alike, and no two fields, or even parts of fields, are alike; and there are no two cultivators who give exactly the same and equal attention to tillage, fertilizing, and the other treatments of plants. All forms or varieties, therefore, tend to "run out" by variation or gradual evolution into other forms; but because we keep the same name for all the succeeding generations, we fancy that we still have the same variety. In 1887 I found a single tomato plant in my garden in Michigan, which had several points of superiority over any other of the one hundred and seventy varieties which I was then growing. It came from a packet of German seed of an inferior variety. The tomato was very solid, an unusually long keeper, productive, and attractive in size and appearance. The variation was so promising that I named it in a sketch of tomatoes which I published that year, calling it the Ignotum (that is, *unknown*), to indicate that the origin of it was no merit of my own. I sent seeds to a few friends for testing. I sowed the seeds for about five hundred plants in 1888 in an isolated patch upon uniform soil. The larger part of the plants were more or less like the parent. A few reverted. A few of the best plants were selected, and the seed saved. I then moved to New York and took the seed with me. This was sown in uniform soil in an isolated position in 1889. This crop, probably as a result of the careful selection of the year before and of the change of locality, was remarkably uniform and handsome. Of the 442 plants which I grew that year, none reverted to the little Eiformige Dauer, the German variety from which it had come, but there was some variation in them due to different methods of treatment. I again saved the seeds, and I was now ready to introduce the variety. I therefore sold my seed, six pounds, to V. H. Hallock & Son, Queens, New York, who introduced it in 1890. The very next year, 1891, I obtained the Ignotum from fifteen dealers and grew the plants side by side. Of the fifteen lots, eight bore small and poor fruits which were not worth growing and which could not be recognized as Ignotum! Grown from our own seed, it still held its characters well. Here, then, only a year after its introduction, half the seedsmen were selling a spurious stock. It is possible that some of this variation arose from substitution of other varieties by seedsmen, although I have yet secured no evidence of any unfair dealing. It is possible, also, that the product of some of the samples which I early sent out for testing had found their way into seedsmen's hands. But I am convinced that very much of this variation was a legitimate result of the various conditions in which the crops of 1890 had been grown, and the varying ideals of those who saved the seeds. I am the more positive of this from the fact that the Ignotum tomato, as I first knew it and bred it, appears to be lost to cultivation, although the name is still used for the legitimate family of descendants from my original stock. All this experience illustrates how quickly varieties pass out by variation and by the unconscious and unlike selection practised by different persons.

The duration of any variety is inversely proportional to the frequency of its generations. Annual plants, other conditions being the same, run out sooner than perennials, because seed-reproduction—or the generations—intervenes more frequently. Trees, on the other hand, carry their variations longer, because the seed-generations—in which departures chiefly take place—are farther apart. Of all the so-called fruit plants, the strawberry runs out soonest and the varieties change the oftenest, because a new generation can be brought into fruit-bearing in two years, whilst it may require a decade or more to bring a new generation of apples or chestnuts into bearing. Yet, my reader will remind me that the Wilson strawberry has been and is the leading variety in many places for nearly forty years, to which I reply that the Wilson of to-day is not necessarily the same as that introduced by James Wilson, simply because the name is the same. Every different soil or treatment tends to produce a different strain or variation in the Wilson strawberry, as it does in any other plant; and every grower, when setting a new plantation, selects his plants from that part of his field which pleases him best, rather than from those plants which most nearly correspond to the original type of the Wilson. That is, this unconscious selection on the part of the grower takes no account of what the variety was, but only of what it ought to be, and this ideal differs with every person. It is not surprising, therefore, to find strains of Wilson strawberry which are as unlike as many named varieties are; and it is to be expected that all of the strains now in existence have departed considerably from the original type.

This example borrowed from the strawberry is a most important one, because it illustrates how a variety may vary and pass out of existence even though it is propagated wholly asexually, or by buds. There are to-day several different types of Rhode Island Greening apple in cultivation, which have originated from variations produced by environment and by the different models which propagators have had in mind; and the same is true of many other fruits.

All the foregoing remarks demonstrate the importance of constant attention to selection if one desires to maintain the exact type of any variety which he has produced. They explain the value of the "roguing"—or systematic destruction of all "rogues" or non-typical plants—which is invariably practised by all good seedgrowers. But they still more emphatically show that every variety is essentially unstable, and that the only abiding result is constant evolution, the old forms being left behind as the type expands into new and better strains. Varieties to be valuable, therefore, ought not to be rigidly fixed, and, fortunately, nature has prescribed that they cannot be. Probably every decade sees a complete change in every variety of any annual species which is propagated exclusively from seeds, and every century must see a like change in the tree fruits. These changes are so gradual, and the original basis of comparison fades away so completely, that we generally fail to recognize the evolution.

15. *It is evident, therefore, that the most abiding progress in the amelioration of plants must come as a result of the very best cultivation and the most intelligent selection and change of seed.* Every reflective person must admit that the cultivation of plants—which is the fundamental conception of agriculture—has been and is crude and imperfect,

and that there has been no conscious effort on the part of the human race to produce any given final result upon the cultivated flora. Yet, this imperfect cultivation has already modified plants so profoundly that we cannot determine the originals of many of them, and we can trace the evolution of but few. The science of rural industry is now fairly well understood in its essential fundamental principles, and the intelligence of those classes of persons who deal with plants is rapidly enlarging. The opening of the twentieth century will virtually mark a new era for agriculture, and from that time on the onward evolution of plants should proceed confidently and unchecked. Our eyes are too often dazzled by the novelties which suddenly thrust themselves upon us, and we look for some mystic power which shall enable us to produce varieties forthwith at our will. We need not so much varieties with new names as we do a general increase in productiveness and efficiency of the types which we already possess ; and this augmentation must come chiefly in the form of a gradual evolution under the stimulus of good care. The man who will accomplish most for the amelioration and unfolding of the forms of plants, is he who fixes his eyes steadily upon the future, and with the inspiration of a long forecast, urges the betterment of all conditions in which plants grow.

III. Specific Examples.

The foregoing principles and discussions will become more concrete if a few actual examples of the origination of varieties are given. In order to begin with a very simple case, I will relate the introduction of the varieties of dewberries, for this fruit is yet little cultivated, the varieties are few, and the domestication of it is not yet thirty years old.

The Dewberry and Blackberry.

The dewberries are native fruits, and it is only within the last ten years that they have become prominent among fruit-growers. The most important one is the Lucretia. This was found growing wild upon a plantation in West Virginia in war time. In 1876, a few of the plants were sent to Ohio, and from this start the present stock has come. It is probable that similar wild varieties are growing to-day in many parts of the country, but they have not chanced to have been seen by persons who are interested in cultivating them. It is a form of the common wild dewberry, which grows all over the northeastern states. Just why this particular patch in West Virginia should have been so much better than the general run of the species, nobody knows, but it was undoubtedly the product of some local environment of soil or position.

K

Early in the seventies, T. C. Bartel, of Huey, Clinton Co., Illinois, observed very excellent dewberries growing in rows between the lines of stubble in an old cornfield, where the plant had evidently been quick to avail itself of unoccupied land. This was introduced as the Bartel dewberry, and is now the second in point of prominence amongst the cultivated varieties. Other varieties have appeared in much the same way. A fruit-grower in Michigan found an extra good dewberry in a neighboring wood-lot, and introduced it under the name of Geer, in compliment to the owner of the place. In Florida, an unusually good plant of the common wild dewberry of that region was discovered, and introduced by Reasoner Brothers, under the name of Manatee. There are now about twenty named varieties of dewberries in cultivation, as described in our horticultural writings, all of which, so far as I know, are chance plants from the wild.

As the dewberries become more widely grown, good seedlings will now and then appear in cultivated ground, and these will be named and sold. After a time persons will begin to sow seeds for the purpose of producing new varieties; and those seedlings which chance to possess unusual merit will be propagated, and in due time introduced. This is the history of the cultivated blackberries and raspberries which have come from the wild plants in less than half a century. These fruits are now so far developed that we no longer think of looking to the woods and copses for new varieties of promise, but the novelties are mostly chance seedlings from cultivated varieties. A few years ago a friend purchased plants of the Snyder blackberry. When they came into bearing he noticed that one plant was better than the rest. It bore larger fruits, and the bearing season was longer. He took suckers from this plant, and from these others were taken, until he now has a large plantation of the novelty, mostly selected from plants which pleased him best. The variety has such distinct merit that I have named it the Mersereau, in honor of the man who recognized and propagated it. He will continue selecting from the best plants, as he propagates year by year, and it may be that in a few years he will have so much improved it that it will no longer be the variety with which he started.

The Apple.

The original apple is not definitely known, but it was certainly a very small and inferior, crabbed fruit, borne mostly in clusters. When we first find it described by historians, it was still of small value. Pliny said that some kinds were so sour as to take the edge off a knife. But better and better seedlings continued to come up about habitations, until, when printed descriptions of fruits began to be made, three or four hundred years ago, there were many named kinds in existence. The size had vastly improved, and with this increase came the reduction of the number of fruits in the cluster; so that, at the present time, whilst apple flowers are borne in clusters, the fruits are generally borne singly. That is, most of the flowers fail to set fruit, and they complete their mission when they have shed their pollen for the benefit of the one which persists.

The American colonists brought with them the staple varieties of the mother countries. But the needs of the new country were unlike those of the old, and the tastes and fashions of the people were changing. So, as seedlings came up about the buildings and along the fences, where the seeds had been scattered, the ones which promised to satisfy the new needs best were saved, and many of the old varieties were allowed to pass away. In 1817, the date of the first American fruit-book, over sixty per cent of the varieties particularly recommended for cultivation in this country were of American origin. In 1845, nearly two hundred varieties of apples were described as having been fruited in this country, of which over half were of American origin. Between these two dates, introductions of foreign varieties had been freely made, so that the percentage of domestic varieties had fallen. But the next thirty years saw a great change. Of 1823 varieties described in 1872, nearly or quite seventy per cent were American, and a still greater proportion of the most prized kinds were of domestic origin. In the older states, the apple had now become so thoroughly accustomed to its environment, and the tastes of the people were so well supplied, that there was no longer much need for the introduction of foreign kinds. It was not so in the Northwest. There the apples of the eastern states did not thrive. The climate was too cold and too dry. Attention was turned to other countries with similar or rigorous climate. In 1870, the Department of Agriculture at Washington imported cions of many varieties of apples from Russia; but these did not satisfy many fruit-growers of the northern states. It was then conceived that the great interior plain of Russia should yield apples adapted to the upper Mississippi valley, whilst those already imported had come from the seaboard territory. Accordingly, early in the eighties, Charles Gibb, of the province of Quebec, and Professor Budd, of Iowa, went to Russia to introduce the promising fruits of the central plain. The result has been a most interesting one to the pacific looker-on. There are ardent advocates of the Russian varieties, and there are others who see nothing good in them. There are those who believe that all progress must come by securing seedlings from the hardiest varieties of the eastern states; there are others who would derive everything from the Siberian crabs, and still others who believe that the final result lies in improving the native crabs. There is no end of discussion and cross-purposes. In the meantime, nature is quietly doing the work. Here is a good seedling of some old variety, there a good one from some Russian, and now and then one from the crab stocks. The new varieties are gradually supplanting the old, so quietly that few people are aware of it; and by the time the contestants are done disputing, it will be found that there are no Russians and no eastern apples, but a brood of northwestern apples which have grown out of the old confusion.

All these new apples are simply seedlings, almost all of them chance trees which come up here and there wherever man has allowed nature a bit of ground upon which to make garden as she likes. In 1892, there were 878 varieties of apples offered for sale by American nurserymen, and it is doubtful if one in the whole lot was the result of any attempt on the part of the originator to produce a variety with definite qualities. And what is true of the apple, is about equally true of the other tree fruits. In the small fruits and the grapes, where the generations are shorter and the results quicker, more has been done in the way of direct selection of seeds and the crossing of chosen parents; but even here, the methods are mostly haphazard.

Beans.

Perhaps there are no plants more tractable in the hands of the plant-breeder than the garden beans. Some two or three years ago, a leading eastern seedsman conceived of a new form of bean pod which would at once commend itself to his customers. He was so well convinced of the merits of this prospective variety, that he made a descriptive and "taking" name for it. He then wrote to a noted bean-raiser, describing the proposed variety and giving the name. "Can you make it for me?" he asked. "Yes, I will make you the bean," replied the grower. The seedsman then announced in his catalogue that he would soon introduce a new bean, and, in order to hold the name, he published it, along with the announcement. Two years later, I visited the bean-grower. "Did you get the bean?" I asked. "Yes, here it is." Sure enough, he had it, and it answered the requirements very well. Another seedsman would like a round-podded, stringless, green-podded bean. This same man produced it, and I went into a field of fifteen acres of it, where it was growing for seed, and the most fastidious person could not have asked for a closer approach to the ideal which the breeder had set before him some four or five years before.

How is all this done? It looks simple enough. The ideal is established first of all. The breeder revolves it in his mind, and eliminates all the impracticable and contradictory elements of it. Then he goes carefully and critically through his bean fields, particularly those varieties which are most like the desired kind, and marks those plants which most nearly approach his ideal The seeds of these are carefully saved, and they are planted in isolated positions. If he finds no promising variations amongst his plantations, then he must start off the variation in some other way. This is usually done by crossing those varieties which are most like the proposed kind. He has got a start; but now the science and skill begin. Year by year he selects just those plants which please him best and which he judges, from experience, will most surely carry their features over to the offspring. He starts with one plant; the next year he may have only two. If he has ten or twenty good ones, then the task is an easy one, for the variety has elements of permanence — that is, of hereditability — in it. But he may have no plants the second year. In that case, he begins again; for if the ideal is true, it can be attained. This bean-breeder to whom I have referred, and upon whom many of our best seedsmen rely for new varieties, tells me that he has discarded fully three thousand varieties and forms as profitless. This only means that he is a most astute judge of beans, and that he knows when any type is likely to prove to be a poor breeder.

The bean also affords an excellent example of the care which it is generally necessary to exercise to keep any variety true to the type. The person of whom I have spoken, in common with all careful seed-growers, searches his field with great pains to discover the "rogues," or those plants which vary perceptibly from the type of the given variety. The rogue may be a variation in size or habit of plant, season of maturity, color or form of pods, productiveness, susceptibility to rust, or other aberrance. In the dwarf or bush beans, which are now most exclusively grown, the most frequent rogue is a climbing or half-climbing plant. This is a reversion to the ancestral type of the bean, which was no doubt a twining plant. This rogue is always destroyed, even though it may be, itself, a good bean. In some cases, the men who perform the roguing are sent along every row of a whole field on their hands and knees, critically examining every plant. The effect of this continual selection is always to push on the variety to greater excellence. The various "improved" strains of plants are obtained in essentially this fashion. If the grower has been painstaking with his roguing, he soon finds that his seed gives better and more uniform crops than the common stock of the variety. If the improvement is marked, he may dignify his strain with a distinct name, and it thereby becomes a new variety. The improvement may be a very important one to a careful bean-grower, and at the same time be so slight as to escape the attention of the general farmer, or even of experimenters who are not particularly skilled in judging the merits of beans.

All these examples drawn from the bean are excellent illustrations of the best and most scientific plant-breeding, and the same methods — varied to suit the different needs — apply to the amelioration of all other plants. The recent dwarf Lima beans may be cited as examples of accidental or fortuitous varieties, in which the preconstructed ideal of the plant-breeder had no place. Four or five of these beans have attained some prominence. Henderson and Kumerle dwarf Limas were introduced in 1889, Burpee in 1890, and Barteldes in 1892 or 1893. The variety which is now called the Henderson was picked up twenty or more years ago by a negro, who found it growing along a roadside in Virginia. It was afterwards grown in various gardens, and about 1885 it fell into the hands of a seedsman in Richmond. Henderson purchased the stock of it in 1887, grew it in 1888, and offered it to the general public in 1889. The introduction of Henderson's bean attracted the attention of Asa Palmer, of Kennett Square, Pennsylvania, who had also been growing a dwarf Lima. He called upon Burpee, the well-known seedsman of Philadelphia, described his variety, and left four beans for trial. These were planted in the test grounds and were found to be valuable. Mr. Palmer's entire stock was then purchased, — comprising over an acre, which had been carefully inspected during the season — and Burpee Bush Lima was presented to the public in the spring of 1890. Mr. Palmer's dwarf Lima originated in 1883, when his entire crop of Large White (Pole) Limas was destroyed by cut-worms. He went over his field to remove the poles before fitting the land for other uses, but he found one little plant, about ten inches high, which had been cut off about an inch above the ground but which had re-rooted. It bore three pods, each containing one seed. These three seeds were planted in 1884, and two of the plants were dwarf, like the parent. By discarding all plants which had a tendency to climb, in succeeding crops, the Burpee Bush Lima, as we now have it, was developed. The Kumerle, Thorburn, or Dreer, Dwarf Lima originated from occasional dwarf forms of the Challenger Pole Lima, which J. W. Kumerle, of Newark, New Jersey, found growing in his field. The stock which came from these selected dwarf plants was introduced by Thorburn and Dreer, under their respective names. The singular Barteldes Bush Lima came from Colorado, and is a similar dwarf sport of the old White Spanish or Dutch Runner bean. Barteldes received about a peck of the seed and introduced it sparingly. It attracted very little attention, and as the following season was dry, Barteldes himself failed to get a crop, and the variety was lost to the trade.

Cannas.

Few plants have shown more remarkable evolutions in very recent years than the cannas. At the present time, the Crozy cannas — so named from Crozy, of Lyons, France, who has introduced the greater number of them — are most popular. This type is often called the French Dwarf, or the Flowering Canna, and it is marked by a comparatively low stature, and very large and showy spreading flowers in many colors, whereas the cannas of a few years ago were very tall plants, with small and late dull red, narrow flowers, and they were grown exclusively for their foliage effects. How has this transformation come about?

In the first place, it should be said that there are many species of canna, and about a half dozen of these were well known to gardeners at the opening of the century. About 1830, the cannas began to attract much attention from cultivators, and the original species were soon variously hybridized. Crossed seeds, and seeds from the successive generations of hybrids, introduced a host of new and variable forms. The first distinct fashion in cannas seems to have been for tall, late-flowering forms. In 1848, Année, a cultivator in France, sowed seeds of Canna Nepalensis, a tall oriental species, and there sprung up a race of plants which has since been known as Canna Annæi. It is probable that this Canna Nepalensis had become fertilized with other species growing in Année's collection, very likely with Canna glauca. At any rate, this race of cannas became popular, and was to its time what the French dwarfs are to the present day. The plants were freely introduced into parks, beginning about 1856, but their use began to wane by 1870 or before. Descendants of this type, variously crossed and modified, are now frequently seen in parks and gardens.

The beginning of the modern race of dwarf, large-flowered cannas was in 1863, when one of the smaller-flowered Costa Rican species (Canna Warscewiczii) was crossed upon a large-flowered

Peruvian species (Canna iridiflora). The offspring of this union came to be called Canna Ehemanni. This hybrid has been again variously crossed with other species, and modified by cultivation and selection, until the present composite type is the result. Seeds give new varieties; and any seedling which is worth saving is thereafter multiplied by divisions of the root, and the resulting plants are introduced to commerce.

These various examples are but types of what has been and can be accomplished in a given group of plants. There is nothing mysterious about the subject, so far as the cultivator is concerned. He simply sets his ideal, makes sure that it does not contradict any of the fundamental laws of development of the plant with which he is to work, then patiently and persistently keeps at his task. He must have good judgment, skill, and inspiration, but he does not need genius.

"In the improvement of plants," writes Henri L. de Vilmorin, "the action of man, much like influences which act on plants in the wild state, only brings about slow and gradual changes, often scarcely noticeable at first. But if the efforts toward the desired end be kept on steadily, the changes will soon become greater and greater, and the last stages of the improvement will become much more rapid than the first ones."

LECTURE IV.

BORROWED OPINIONS; BEING EXTRACTS FROM THE WRITINGS OF B. VERLOT, E. A. CARRIÈRE, AND W. O. FOCKE.

I. VERLOT'S CLASSIFICATION OF VARIETIES OF ORNAMENTAL PLANTS.

VERLOT (*Sur la Production et la Fixation des Variétés dans les Plantes d'Ornement*) distributes the varieties of ornamental plants into sixteen groups. I shall now transcribe these groups, and under each shall give a very brief quotation or abstract of some of his remarks concerning them.

1. *Varieties distinguished by diminution of stature, or dwarfing.* — Dwarfing is one of the most frequent variations in the vegetable kingdom, but, unlike many similar phenomena in the animal kingdom, these dwarfs are nearly always very fertile. If we question the cultivators upon the subject, they respond that these variations are purely accidental, and that whenever the variations offer any reward they are propagated and distributed.

Dwarfing may be brought about by sowing the seeds in the autumn (page 115), and at the same time successively transplanting the plants, as they need. Suppose, for example, we sow seeds of Coreopsis tinctoria in August or September. When the plants have developed leaves, they are transplanted, leaving sufficient space between them to allow of liberal growth. When the plants begin to touch each other, transplant again, perhaps three or even four times. The plants become strong, vigorous, and stocky; we encourage the development of the lowest branches and thereby tend to shorten the leading stem, thus making the individual comparatively dwarf. The seeds saved from plants thus treated during several generations will be more apt to produce dwarf varieties than seeds taken from other plants. The greater part of dwarf varieties appear in those plants which are sown in autumn, and in those, if sown in spring, which are submitted to successive transplantings. Thus, amongst the annual species which we habitually sow in July and September, the following have produced dwarf varieties: —

> Calceolaria plantaginea.
> Senecio cruentus.
> Lychnis (or Agrostemma) Cœli-rosa.
> Coreopsis (or Calliopsis) tinctoria.
> Œnothera Drummondii.
> Helichrysum bracteatum.
> Leptosiphon densiflorus.

Dianthus Chinensis.
Scabiosa atropurpurea.
Schizanthus retusus.
Iberis umbellata.

Amongst those species which we sow in spring, but frequently transplant, the following have dwarf forms: —

Impatiens Balsamina.
Callistephus hortensis.
Tagetes patula.
Tagetes erecta.
Tagetes signata.

2. *Varieties distinguished by augmentation of stature, or giant forms.* — These varieties result from various causes, amongst which are amount and fertility of soil, the employment of newly harvested seeds, and crossing.

3. *Hardy varieties.* — These are produced by successive selections from the most hardy individuals. Hardy races are also obtained by crossing with hardy species or types. Thus, the forms of Rhododendron arboreum are rendered hardier when crossed with R. Catawbiense.

4. *Large-flowered varieties.* — These variations are always due to a good soil which is rich in humus, and above all by thorough and intelligent cultivation. These are easily fixed, but they pass away

insensibly when the conditions under which they were produced are neglected. This return to small flowers is well illustrated in the pansy. [All plants which are grown for the beauty of their flowers tend to increase the size of those organs, because of the vigor which comes of good care, and the selection which necessarily follows. The frequency of the varietal name "grandiflora" is proof of this. As soon as the plant has made any perceptible gain in the size of its flowers, some nurseryman adds this adjective to its name, as in Hydrangea paniculata grandiflora. No doubt the name is sometimes bestowed without warrant, for the purpose of selling the plant. Frequently the catalogue-maker drops the proper specific name and uses the varietal adjective as if it were the legitimate name of the plant, as in Gazania grandiflora, which is properly Gazania rigens, variety grandiflora.]

5, 6. *Early and late varieties.* — The chief agency affecting the duration of plants is climate, and desired variations in earliness or lateness are obtained by transporting the plants to those climates which produce such effects as we seek, and growing them there for a time; or we can procure seeds from such climates, if the given plants are already grown there.

The age of the seed also has an influence upon the resulting individual: the fresher the seed, the more rapid its germination, and consequently the more prompt the development of the plant. We have reason to expect that fresh seeds will have a tendency to produce early varieties, and that, on the contrary, old seeds, by germinating more slowly, will produce variations more or less late. [Not only does the age of the seed seem to be important in this connection, but recent experiments seem to show that the degree of maturity also modifies the offspring. Seeds which are barely ripe enough to germinate have a tendency to give earlier progeny than those which are fully matured and ripened. See page 103.]

The first seeds to mature on any plant may be expected to give early plants, and the subsequent seeds give later plants. [Verlot states that a cold region tends to make the plants later when transferred to it, but this seems to be an error. The fact is generally just the reverse. Plants taken towards the poles or to higher altitudes, become earlier in two ways, by shortening their period of growth, and by vegetating at a less sum-temperature in spring. See page 26.]

7. *Odoriferous varieties.* — Odor varies greatly, even amongst varieties of one species. The causes of the differences in fragrance are not numerous and they are little understood. Climate, exposure, and the nature of the soil are leading factors. The odor of plants which grow on dry and arid

hills is much more penetrating than that of the same species cultivated in humid and shady places. It is possible, even, to entirely change the odor by transporting the plant from one place to another. For example, Satyrium hircinum exhales a most pronounced goat-like odor in the vicinity of Paris and northward, whilst in the east, and particularly in the southern regions, its flowers have an odor which is somewhat like that of vanilla.

8. *Varieties with colored parts.*—Coloration may be either complete or partial, and it may reside in any or all parts of the plant, as follows:—

> The stems.
> The leaves.
> The flowers, { variegated, spotted.
> The fruits.
> The seeds.

Variations in color are the most frequent of all modifications in cultivated plants. These departures may be expected to arise under the influence of continued cultivation and repeated sowings; and the variations must then be selected until they are fixed.

9. *Varieties without color, or albinos.*—Partial albinism, or variegation, is as frequently observed in spontaneous plants as it is in cultivated ones. It usually occurs in the leaves only, but it is some-

times a feature of the entire plant. A variegated plant does not exist of which we do not know the non-variegated type. These variegated plants appear both from seeds and from bud-variations, and they are most surely propagated in the latter case. It has been said that when the albinism affects the margin of the leaf it is more likely to be transmitted than when it occupies the central part of the blade, but this generalization has many exceptions. Page 157.

It is a curious fact that variegation and doubleness of flowers are generally antagonistic, for they do not appear in the same plant. One excludes the other. It is supposed by Morren [and generally accepted] that doubling is the result of excessive vigor and that partial albinism comes of an enfeebling of the vital functions.

Variegations sometimes disappear entirely and then, after two or three years, reappear in the same individual. The first leaves of seedlings from variegated plants may be perfectly green, and the seedlings may afterwards take on the variegated character. This behavior is well marked in some ferns.

Complete albinism, or chlorosis, indicates a profound alteration in the tissues, and it is impossible of propagation. This decoloration is most commonly a bud-variation.

10. *Double varieties, or those distinguished by*

the transformation of the stamens and pistils into petaloid organs — There are various degrees of doubling or duplication in flowers. The calyx and corolla alone may be duplicated, in which case the flower is still fertile. Sometimes the stamens only are transformed into petal-like organs, and the flower is then fertile if pollen is transferred from another flower. Sometimes all the floral series — calyx, corolla, stamens, pistils — may be duplicated or transformed; then we have a full (*pleine*) flower, which is incapable of producing seeds or of fecundating another flower. [Annual plants, and others not propagated by buds and other asexual parts, which bear full double flowers, must be propagated by seeds taken from flowers which are nearly full double, but which bear a few seeds; or, sometimes from a nearly single flower which is fertilized by pollen from a nearly full double flower. In these cases, it is unusual for all the seedlings to produce full double flowers.]

A rich soil, a cultivation which produces a luxuriant vegetation, are the conditions which generally produce doubling in flowers. But we can repeat with De Candolle, " That if we are generally ignorant of the causes of the doubling of flowers, we also know that if we gather seeds from an individual with semi-double flowers, the plants which result have a greater tendency to produce double flowers than seeds taken from simple flowers."

Doubling may occur in all plants, whether annuals, biennials, herbaceous or woody perennials, and in all of them, when they are fertile, we can finally make them reproduce the character identically.

We must always choose for seed-parents the individuals of which the flowers are very double, and exclude with the greatest care the single-flowered plants, which are the most fertile and the progeny of which quickly smother the progeny of the double flowers.

11. *Proliferous varieties.* — [These are variations which are characterized by growths arising from unusual places, as one flower springing out of another flower, a branch or rosette growing out of a flower, an unusual production of bulbs or young plants from the root, bulbs from leaves or the fronds of ferns, and the like.] These forms are infrequent in cultivated plants and very rare amongst wild plants. They are generally associated with the fertility of the soil. The proliferous form of Papaver somniferum known as Papaver monstruosum, perpetuates itself perfectly by seeds, but these variations are usually unstable.

12. *Varieties with conjoined parts (variétés par soudures).* — We know of a single example of this

monstrosity in ornamental plants: it is that of Papaver bracteatum, in which the corolla has become monopetalous by the growing together of the petals. This monstrosity (described and figured in *Revue Horticole*) is cultivated by Vilmorin. They can propagate it only by cuttings. They have tried in vain to multiply it by seeds. [Similar forms of other species are known.]

12. *Abortive varieties.* — This type of monstrosity, which constitutes one of the most interesting chapters in vegetable teratology, has been observed in all parts of the flower. They are malformations which have no interest from the point of view of ornament. [The petals, or other organs, sometimes almost entirely disappear in this type of variations.]

14. *Peloric varieties.* — [Peloria is a name applied by Linnæus to a form of the toad-flax, Linaria vulgaris, in which all of the five petals have spurs, while the normal form has only one petal spurred. The term is now applied generically to all similar regularity of structure in normally irregular flowers.] The causes which produce this transformation are not known, but aridity and dryness of the soil, and new conditions of vegetation, appear to favor its development. These monstrosities, at least in linaria, are propagated easily by cuttings or buds, and Willdenow records an experiment in which they came true from seeds.

15. *Chloranthic varieties.* — Here are included, in a general way and in lieu of a better name, all those transformations which render the flowers absolutely sterile, and transform them more or less completely into branches or leaf-like organs. They are purely bud-variations, and can be perpetuated only by cuttings, buds, or other asexual parts.

16. *Various* or *polymorphous varieties*, comprising the following types: —

STEMS
- thornless,
- spineless,
- fastigiate,
- filiform,
- weeping, etc.

LEAVES
- crisped,
- fasciated,
- bullate or blistered,
- laciniate, etc.

The various modifications originate both by seed-variation and bud-variation.

II. CARRIÈRE'S ACCOUNT OF BUD-VARIETIES.

The subject of bud-variations or sports never fails to interest the student, and however familiar he may be with these forms he never ceases to wonder at them. I have taken pains, therefore, in addition to what I have already said upon the subject (see pages 28, 117), to translate almost bodily Carrière's account of bud-varieties (in *Production et Fixation des Variétés dans les Végétaux*), because, although written in 1865, it is the most extended list of bud-varieties which I know. The catalogue might be greatly extended by inserting the current varieties in commerce in this country, but the original list is sufficiently full for all purposes of illustration. Carrière's account now follows: —

1. *General Remarks upon Bud-Variation.*

Plants being composed of a certain number of elements disposed in a certain order, and, moreover, these elements, under the influence of organic laws, being able to separate or group themselves in different ways, it follows that the same plant can, upon its different parts, present characters and properties more or less different from those which it normally presents. It is this fact which constitutes that which in practice we call an accident [or bud variety], either of dimorphism[1] [of form] or of dichroism [of color].

[1] French writers use the word *accident* in the sense in which we use bud-variation. The word *dimorphism*, used by Carrière for one of the features of bud-variation, is now applied to

We refer to bud-variation the phenomenon, whose cause is unknown, which allows a bud on any part of the plant to develop a member whose form and appearance differ from those borne on other parts of the plant. Thus the common beech producing a branch with laciniate leaves, Podocarpus Koraiana producing a branch whose ramifications are whorled and spreading instead of being scattered, and whose leaves are distichous instead of being alternately disposed about the branches as they are normally, are examples of bud-varieties.

Taken in its most absolute sense and considered in the sum of all its characters, bud-variation, aside from the details which it presents, can be divided into two sections: one which includes all the phenomena which are manifested suddenly, as in the case of the fern-leaved beech, the hemp-leaved rose, the English willow-leaved cherry, sour grapes with long seeds, etc.; the other includes all slower transformations, as in the case of Rosa Eglanteria, tulips, Iris Xiphium, Viola Rothomagensis, var. pallida, etc. Strictly, we could establish a third section to include all the transformations resulting from the age of the individ-

different permanent and characteristic forms of individuals of the same species. It is most commonly observed in the different relative lengths of stamens and pistils. I have substituted other words for it in most places in the text. — L. H. B.

ual, which are the consequences of its adultness. However, this last series of phenomena is seen only in polymorphous species, which change in appearance, form, and nature when they grow old and especially when they bear fruit; such are the ivies, Ficus stipulata or scandens, eucalyptus, etc. Horticulture often profits by this peculiar property of plants; multiplying separately the parts with the exceptional characters, it obtains individuals which present an appearance different from the plants from which they arise. [This dissimilarity between young and mature individuals of the same species is well marked in some of the Coniferæ, as the cedars and retinosporas.]

In a general way, then, dimorphism refers to a different form on the same individual, whether the change be complete or partial. Dichroism is exactly analogous to it in essential points, only that it refers to color instead of to form. Thus, Flon's Pink [Dianthus semperflorens of gardens, introduced by M. Flon of Angers], which has red flowers, developing a branch similar to the plant in aspect and form, but bearing white flowers, the ovate-leaved privet and the Japanese fusain [Euonymus Japonicus] producing buds giving rise to variegated leaves, white kidney-beans producing black ones, and *vice versa*, are examples of dichroism.

Let us say that in bud-variation, less than anywhere else, we can do nothing towards obtaining or producing the variations. Bud-varieties most often spring up spontaneously, so to speak, and in this respect our work is purely passive, consisting in superintending these digressions or accidents in the endeavor to take advantage of them when they are presented. Let us state, also, that in these series of varieties we find a considerable diversity, either in the habit or aspect of the plants or in their foliage or flowers, or sometimes even in their fruits, and that we oftener find variegations than among plants which come from seeds.

We ought to recall just here,—what we have said on the subject of plants issuing from seeds,—that variegations are the more constant the more completely they circumscribe the organs upon which they occur, whether upon the flowers or the leaves; also, that when, on a plant whose variegations are disposed in stripes or bands, we find a part upon which they are disposed circularly, we can be almost certain that, if we detach and graft or make a cutting of this part, we shall preserve its new character. This phenomenon is very frequent in the camellias and especially in the azaleas. The greater part of the varieties of azalea which present these characters have had no other origin.[1]

[1] To preserve variegations, it is best to resort to graftage, generally speaking, as cuttings tend to produce individuals more vigorous, and which therefore tend to return to the green

Certain species are much more disposed than others to produce these bud-varieties, either of dimorphism or dichroism. We give an example from the Chinese chrysanthemum. About 1836, the horticultural establishment of Fromont received from England three varieties of this chrysanthemum; one had the flowers red, one variegated, and one white flesh-colored. Planted in the open air, the following year we saw the three varieties on one plant, which seems to show that these three varieties were only sports from a common form. A phenomenon analogous to the preceding, and which, like it, concerns the Chinese chrysanthemum, was shown at the Museum[1] in 1856 upon a variety called Surprise. This, which bore flowers scarcely rose flesh-colored, produced, on one of its branches, flowers of a deep rose-lilac. Cuttings having been made, it has preserved all its characters, and to-day it is still one of the most beautiful of the section. We call it Gain du Muséum. In 1862, upon this same Gain du Muséum, a branch developed which bore flowers perfectly white, of almost the same size and form as those of the type; then upon dif-

color, or even to the normal form, if the variety differs also in form. We must select the parts, in perpetuating variegations, in which the variegation is very pronounced, although we must exercise care that the variegation be not too intense, else the offspring will be weak and poor. — CARRIÈRE. (See page 149.)

[1] Muséum d'Histoire Naturelle de Paris.

ferent branches beside it were found others bearing flowers half red, half white. In making cuttings from these two kinds of branches, we would then obtain from the Surprise still other varieties. Let us look at the variety Sophie. This, which has dirty white flowers very slightly tinged with red, with yellow centre, has produced, by bud-variation, a plant known as Trophée. The latter, which has flowers of a rose-lilac-violet, bears some resemblance to the Gain du Muséum. There were also upon the same branch, but on different twigs, flowers similar to those borne by the varieties Trophée and Sophie. These new flowers were flat and had narrow and imbricated petals, whilst the Trophée has convex flowers, large and slightly serrate petals. The Madame Richard chrysanthemum, of which the flowers are whitish very lightly bordered with rose, has produced on one of its branches violet flowers stronger than those of the plant from which it sprung; the petals are also larger and more imbricated. In 1863 we observed on certain varieties of chrysanthemum the following sports: the variety called Cedo nulli, with double white flowers very lightly rose, produced a branch which bore flowers much larger and much more spreading than those of Cedo nulli. The Argentine, with small white flowers, pompon-form, gave a branch more vigorous than itself, whose spreading, very large flowers, of a beautiful yellow, resembled to a certain extent those of the large-flowered chrysanthemum, a fact which tends to show that from the pompons to the large-flowered sorts there is but a step. In 1864 we saw upon a stem of the Vesta (a pompon chrysanthemum which has white flowers) several branches which bore flowers entirely deep yellow. The dimensions, as well as the form of the flowers, were the same.

Varieties obtained by bud-variation are very numerous. There is not a genus among those which comprise a number of species which has not produced them. Although we shall mention, farther on, a certain number of these bud-varieties, adding some observations, there are some which, in our opinion, are so interesting that, by anticipation, we ought to speak of them here. One of them relates to a kind of pink which is known in commerce as Flon's pink. This Flon's pink, which is closely related to those which we call Spanish pink, Badin pink, etc., has flowers very deep red, almost double, so that it does not produce seeds, and we are obliged to multiply it by cuttings. Nevertheless, it has already given, by bud-variation, several varieties, of which the most remarkable, a very beautiful white, was developed in 1858. Since that time this variety has been maintained with all its characters. Obtained by M. Paré, horticulturist at Paris, this variety has been called Marie Paré, for one of the children of the originator. Other varieties, presenting colors different from that of which we have spoken, have been developed from Flon's pink by M. Paré. [The pinks are fertile in bud-varieties, particularly the carnation. Many of the carnations which are now well known to commercial growers first appeared as sports. The Portia, which is a deep self-red, frequently sports, sometimes into almost pure white.]

The genus which, probably, has produced the most examples of this nature is the Rose. The examples are so very interesting that we cannot resist the temptation to say something in detail concerning them. We will cite several remarkable examples, commencing with those which have sprung from the Hundred-leaved Rose [Provence rose, Rosa centifolia]. The bud-varieties which have issued from this rose can be arranged in two series: one which includes all individuals which are but little removed from the type, which differ from it only in color or form, either of the flowers or sometimes of the leaves, and comprise the ordinary Hundred-leaved roses; the other series includes individuals possessing the characters of the first series, but which, in addition, are provided with small bracts or glandular hairs which give the name "Moss-rose." Bud-varieties produced by Rosa centifolia: —

A. Ordinary Hundred-leaved roses.
   I. Flowers more or less large.
      Cabbage-leaved or lettuce-leaved R. centifolia.
      Celery-leaved.
      Anemone.
      Nancy.
      Peintres.
      Flore magno, or *Foliaceous.*
      Apetalous.
      Unique white.
      Unique variegated.
   II. Flowers small.— Pompons.
      Burgogne pompon.
      White pompon.
      Bordeaux pompon.
      Kingston pompon.

B. Moss-roses.
   I. Flowers more or less large.
      Ordinary.
      Cristata.
      White-flowered
      Variegated.
      Sage-leaved.
      Unique Provence.
      Zoé, or *Mousseuse partout.*
   II. Flowers small. — Pompons.
      Pompon.

One must not suppose that all the moss-roses which he meets with to-day in commerce are the result of bud-variation. The larger part, on the contrary, come from seeds. The moss-rose is nearly a race. From seeds taken from the moss-rose, we have obtained a certain number of individuals which have preserved the general characters of the plants from which they came; they are more or less "mossy." Let us state, however, that this "mossy" character is not peculiar to any section of roses, but that we find it in most garden species, as the hybrid remontants, rose-of-four-seasons, etc. The fact of the reproduction of the "mossiness" of roses by seeds, proves again, what we have asserted several times, that everything in a plant tends to reproduce itself, that the peculiarities, properties, monstrosities even, may become hereditary.

The Zoé moss-rose is one of the most remarkable bud-varieties which has been produced by Rosa centifolia. This variety, instead of being "mossy" only upon the peduncle or calyx, as most of the other varieties of this group are, is "mossy" on all its parts, whence the name *Mousseuse partout*. ["mossy everywhere"]. This variety was produced again in 1864, at M. Jamain's, horticulturist, Paris, where we followed the development of it. We also learned that at this place, in two beds planted with ordinary moss-roses, beside the Zoé, there were several stems which tended likewise to modify themselves, some in their leaves, others in their flowers.

We must remark that it often happens that certain individuals of bud-varieties return, on some one of their parts, to the type from which they came. Thus, on a moss-rose from R. centifolia, we have seen a branch of the ordinary Hundred-leaved rose. We should observe, however, that most usually the parts which seem to return to the type present, notwithstanding, differences from it. There has been a step in advance, and it is contrary to nature to retrace completely.

The Rose du Roi, known by nearly every one, has produced the following six bud-varieties: —

1. Bernard Perpetual. This rose has the branches more slender than those of the parent; its flowers and leaves are also smaller. Its pompon flowers are very pretty, with a rose-color very much brighter than that of the Rose du Roi.

2. Long-peduncled Rose du Roi. This has branches much longer than those of the type; the internodes are more distant, and the peduncles are also longer. It is only a sort of degeneration.

3. Madame Tellier. Very similar to the last, being distinguished only by its flowers, which are less colored, possessing a very bright rose flesh-color.

4. Mogador. This rose differs from Rose du Roi by its stronger flowers, of a more vivid, deeper red; its branches more colored, permitting it to be distinguished even in winter. Horticulturists do not like this variety, because it is hard to force, and because it passes very quickly to a dirty violet.

5. Capitaine Renard, or Variegated Rose du Roi. This variety differs from Madame Tellier by its flowers being variegated or ribboned with white. It was found at Orleans by M. Desfossé-Thuillier.

6. Cœlina Dubos. Found by M. Dubos, horticulturist at Pierrefitte, near Saint-Denis, upon Rose du Roi. It has the branches more slender and the leaves a little smaller than the parent; its flowers, very similar in form to those of the type, are white, slightly flesh-colored.

The Rose de la Reine has produced two sports: one, Belle Normande, whose flowers, rose flesh-colored, recall those of Souvenir de la Malmaison; the other, Madame Cambel of Isly, or Triomphe de Valenciennes, which differs from the parent only in its marbled-variegated flowers.

The Duchesse de Cambacérès rose, which has uni-colored, deep rose flowers, has produced by bud-variation Belle de Printemps, which has rose flowers marbled with brown.

The Baronne Prévost has produced, to our

knowledge, five varieties, two of which have variegated flowers and one marbled. One of the two variegated varieties, Madame Désirée Giraud, was found at the place of M. Désiré Giraud at Marly, near Valenciennes. It is not vigorous. The second variety, Panachée d'Orléans, which was observed for the first time at Orléans, is very vigorous. Its branches are more slender than those of Baronne Prévost, and the very smooth and shiny bark has few prickles. In short, its branches recall those of Cuisse de Nymphe. It sometimes happens that this variety produces large branches, vigorous and very thorny, but less so than those of Baronne Prévost; its flowers also resemble the type more closely. It is an intermediate produced by the single matter of vegetation. The Baronne Prévost marbré differs from the type only in its flowers, which are marbled with brown. Another variety, placed in the trade by M. Pierre Oger, horticulturist at Caen, differs from the type only in the color of the flowers, which are very much paler. The fifth sport produced by the Baronne Prévost is more recent. We observed it first in 1864, at Vitry-sur-Seine, in a garden under the care of M. Lachaume. We called it Madame Lachaume. It differs from the type by its branches being a little less thorny, but especially by its inflorescence, which, long-paniculate, very much branched, recalls that of certain Noisettes. The flower, also, is a little weaker than that of the type. But a very remarkable fact is that the hip, instead of being very regularly attenuated at its base and becoming confounded with the peduncle, as in Baronne Prévost, is abruptly and slightly inflated, then contracted, and inflated again near the summit. The peduncles are also much more slender and longer than those of the parent.

The Duchesse d'Orléans, whose flowers are violet-rose, produced by bud-variation, in 1858, a variety known as Sœur des Anges. This variety differs from its parent particularly in the color of the flowers, which is pale flesh-rose, like that of the flowers of Souvenir de la Malmaison.

The rose called Quatre-Saisons has produced the following sports: —

1. White Moss, or de Thionville. This was first observed at Thionville about 1835. It differs from the type by its branches being more slender and supplied with hispid, glandular hairs. Its light green leaves are also softer to the touch and slightly tomentose. Its flowers are pure white. Sometimes it produces strong branches which bear rose-colored flowers. In this latter condition it is the ordinary Quatre-Saisons, a fact observed by M. Duval of Montmorency. later by M. Victor Verdier, Paris, and recently (1864) at the Museum.

2. Quatre-Saisons pompon.
3. White.

The Provence roses have likewise produced a number of bud-varieties. Among the best known are:—

>Pompon Saint-François.
>Pompon Saint-Jacques.
>Camaieu.
>Panaché semi-double.
>Tricolore de Flandre.

The last variety, which appeared in Belgium some years ago, is remarkable for its variegated flowers; it is a slender grower, although it comes from a very vigorous variety. It sometimes returns to the type. The variety Camaieu is remarkable for its striped flowers, very pretty, and almost unique in the genus. Its wood is meagre and its leaflets are toothed.

In the Damask roses, which are sorts of Quatre-Saisons roses, not remontants, we consider as bud-varieties the three following:—

>Damask York and Lancaster.
>Damask with blistered leaves.

The ordinary Bengal rose has sported into the Bengale à bois strié [striped-stemmed Bengal]. The branches are often almost completely yellow.

A very curious sport of the rose is the plant which we have called Rosier à feuilles de Chanvre [hemp-leaved rose]. By its flowers and especially by its leaves, this variety differs considerably from Rosa alba, from which it comes. Its leaflets are hooded, long and narrow, and very coarsely dentate-serrate, sometimes as if gnawed on the edges, strongly nerved, of a dark green, rugose-scabrous. It happens sometimes, also, that its leaves are opposite upon certain branches. The flowers of this variety are smaller than those of Rosa alba, often irregular, and somewhat monstrous, and always sterile. [Probably no plants are so prolific of bud-varieties as the roses. Every gardener of experience has observed the fact. The following experiences of a single horticulturist (Ernest Walker, New Albany, Indiana), with one rose, illustrate this fact admirably. "I have had a number of sports of the Perle des Jardins rose," he writes me, "in our greenhouses. The first one was a double silvery pink with a short bud, and a very double, somewhat quartered flower. The stock of this I sold, as a new variety, for fifty dollars. The next sport was a white Perle. [The Perle is a golden-yellow rose.] I sold a plant of Perle to a local customer, who afterwards complained that it was not true to name, because the flower was white. She took it to be Cornelia Cook. I went to see the rose, and found a Perle rose in everything but color. I secured the plant, and was intending to introduce it, when, within a few months. I heard that Nanz & Neuner, of Louisville, Kentucky, had one, and that a London firm had another; and later I found that one had originated in Germany. Another sport of Perle was a single rose, like Isabella Sprunt. Another was like a Madame Falcot. At another time a whole branch sported into a form with a long, slender bud (about two inches long and five-eighths inch in diameter), with only two calyx lobes, and only two petals, — which were very broad, — in each cycle or series. This sport was really a monstrosity, and I could not propagate it."]

The so-called ornamental plants are not the only ones which present these examples of heteromorphism. Fruit trees furnish very remarkable examples. We will cite some cases, beginning with those furnished by the cherry called Anglais hâtif [Early English]. The most curious sport given us by this cherry is that which we call Cerisier Anglais hétérophylle or à feuilles de saule [heterophyllous or willow-leaved English cherry]. This is the history of the sport: Upon a young tree whose parts are normal, we see, sometimes suddenly and without apparent cause, a vigorous bud develop, which bud, instead of producing leaves of the ordinary form, bears those which are very long and narrow, often somewhat falcate, and often irregularly erose.

Grafted, this variety presents very singular peculiarities, as follows: so long as it preserves its exceptional characters the plant does not flourish, but as it constantly tends to lose them we observe that when the leaves have almost returned to the normal form the trees flourish and bear. Nevertheless, this variety never resumes identically the characters of the type from which it came. Its aspect is always distinct. The tree is never fertile, and its fruit also differs from that of the Early English. The young shoots preserve their accidental character, and each year the leaves which it develops are nearly identical to those which the variety produced when it was first developed.

This variety is not the only one which is presented by the Early English. Thus, when the trees are old, it frequently happens that we find on the same individual three kinds of fruits, distinct in their times of maturing. There is, first, the Early English, whose fruits become black; the Late English, whose fruits, of a beautiful deep red, shining as if varnished, ripen later. Finally, we nearly always find another variety, very late, whose fruits, a little smaller, are still entirely green when the other two have been gathered a long time. In these three sports, the differences are shown only on the fruits. The Indule cherry is also only a sport from the Early

English. It is distinguished by its foliage and earliness. The Early English cherry is not the only one which furnishes bud-varieties pertaining to the fruits. We find analogous examples in the May Duke, Cherry Duke, and Reine Hortense. These varieties, indeed, have produced on different branches of the same individual subvarieties whose fruits ripened a fortnight later than normally. Grafted, each of these subvarieties preserves its accidental character.

A phenomenon analogous to the preceding ones is shown each year at the Museum upon an ordinary double-flowered cherry. The tree upon which this anomaly was developed is nearly fourteen inches in diameter, is grafted on the Sainte-Lucie about twenty-seven inches above the ground. Above the junction the stem is naked for about six and a half feet. At this height is a large branch, which every year is covered with extremely double flowers, whilst the flowers of other branches, expanding very much later, are scarcely half double, and yield fruits.

The Coé violette plum is an example of dichroism. It is a bud-variety which was produced on the White-fruited Coé, and which, grafted, is maintained with all the characters which it presented at the time of its appearing. We have very often observed upon the Damas de Tours plum an instance almost the same as the preceding. On the same tree there were branches which bore fruits different in form and color, and differing a fortnight in time of maturing. Thus, while the fruits of the type are very large, lengthened, of a deep red color which recalls the Pond Seedling, marked only on one side by a very slight furrow, the fruits of the later sub-variety are a little smaller, and their form is that of the ordinary Reine Claude; they are of an herbaceous green, which passes more or less into a very clear red; the stem, arched, swollen at the base, is inserted in a cavity quite large by the widening of the furrow, whilst the stem of the typical fruits is erect, little or not at all swollen, inserted in a very small cavity placed almost on the surface of the fruit.

Another plum, the Prunier Puget, presents the following peculiarities: Upon the same branch it very frequently happens that there are fruits of a violet-red, dotted or striped with red-green. We find some, also, which present all the intermediate tints and others which are almost unicolored. By multiplying them separately, there may be a chance to establish these varieties and to obtain several from one tree.

We have seen on a red-fruited currant bush a branch which bore fruits as white as those of the Hollande à fruits blancs [White Dutch].

The fact of the nectarine coming suddenly from

a peach can no longer be doubted. Recent examples have come to support the experiments of certain authors, notably Sieulle.

Two other similar examples, of which we ought to speak, are furnished by two varieties of Chasselas grapes, one known as Chasselas panaché [Variegated Chasselas] and Chasselas Suisse [Swiss Chasselas]. Both appear to have come from a variety with black fruits, the color which predominates in them. These are the peculiarities which they present: almost all the bunches bear some fruits more or less variegated or striped, white in Chasselas Suisse, red in Chasselas panaché. But it happens frequently that the elements are separated and that we have then, upon different shoots, sometimes upon the same shoot, bunches of grapes of different color, almost entirely white if they belong to the Chasselas Suisse, and red if they belong to the Chasselas panaché. One of the varieties is only a modification of the other, which is itself only a modification of some other.

The pear Saint-Germain gris, whose deep gray fruits are very different in appearance from those of the ordinary Saint-Germain, is a bud-variety which was produced upon a branch of the latter, and which, multiplied by grafting, is maintained in all its characters. A similar variety was produced on the Messire-Jean, so that at present we possess in the gardens a Messire-Jean gris, and a Messire-Jean jaune [gray and yellow Messire-Jean]. To these examples we will add two other analogous ones, which were recorded in the *Bulletin de l'Académie des Sciences*, xxxiv., meeting of May 17th. One, given by M. Dureau de la Malle, refers to the Bon Chrétien pear, which produced sometimes typical fruits and at others "of a form entirely different and unknown." The other example, cited by M. Mourrière, professor at Bernay, has reference to an apple which, on the same branches, produced fruits which had the appearance of a Reinette rousse and others which resembled a kind of Reinette du Canada. The latter is smooth, punctated, and often of a bright red upon one side. [The recent experiments of Waite, in this country, respecting the immediate influence of pollen, raise the question if some of these minor variations in form of the pear fruit may not have arisen from vagaries of pollination.]

The various examples which we have cited are common to a very large number of plants, among which we will cite the banana and sugar-cane. Indeed, although these plants do not produce seeds, we find in each species a large number of varieties which are very distinct in vigor, aspect, habit, and in the banana in form, size, and quality of fruit. All these varieties are produced by bud-variation. These remarks can be applied to other monocotyledonous plants, as Arundo, Phalaris, Bamboos, Dracaena, Yucca, etc.

[Carrière cites the different shapes and colors of beans in the same pod as examples of bud-variation, but it is a question if these differences are not determined in the seed of the previous year. At all events, since there is only a single year in the life of the bean, we prefer to ascribe variations in it to the generation of the parents from which it has just sprung. There is no previous year's growth of the same individual with which to compare variations and to ascertain if they are bud-departures from the type. Page 118.]

2. *List of Bud-varieties.*[1]

After having sought to present certain examples of bud-variation which, by their importance, seem to be sufficient to fix the attention, we will continue by the enumeration of a certain number of others, without, however, entering into details for each one of them. Sometimes we shall give only the name of the variety. If, however, they present particular interest, either in a practical or scientific point of view, we shall dwell upon them more at length, considering either their origins or peculiarities. [The garden names of the plants

---

[1] The student should also consult Darwin's "Animals and Plants under Domestication."

are given essentially as they stand in the original, for, as the purpose of this list is to acquaint horticulturists with the nature and frequency of bud-variations, I have considered it unnecessary to make any particular attempt to revise the nomenclature. The names are familiar, and, therefore, useful as they stand.]

It would have been easy to extend this enumeration of examples of bud-variation. We have not thought it necessary because, aside from leading us too far, the real interest of the subject would gain nothing by it. We have, then, thought it our duty to put limits upon a subject which has no limits.

Acer eriocarpum, fasciatum.

Very remarkable for its much fasciated branches. This variety showed itself at the Museum in 1857 upon a seedling which, during the first two years, presented nothing abnormal. In the third year, when the tree had been cut back, the sport appeared, since which time it has maintained itself with all its characters. This variety is to A. eriocarpum what the variety montrosa is to Sambucus nigra.

Acorus gramineus, variegata.[1]

[1] When a name is not followed by remarks, the reader is to understand that it represents a known variety and that the name of the species indicates the origin of the variety. — L. H. B.

Æsculus rubicunda, variegata.

[Æsculus Hippocastanum, double-flowered. Upon a well-known Horse Chestnut tree in the environs of Geneva the owner, in 1822 or 1823, detected a single branch bearing double flowers. This still continues to bear double flowers and grafts from it do the same. It is thought to be the original of all the doubled-flowered Horse Chestnuts in the world. — A. De Candolle in *Acad. Sci.*, Paris, 1875, quoted by Asa Gray, *Silliman's Journ.* 3d ser. x. 238].

Agathæa amelloides, variegata.
Ageratum Mexicanum, nanum.

This plant, which is now used to so much advantage for borders, is the product of a branch which developed accidentally from A. Mexicanum. Its heads are almost sessile and a little irregular, borne so close to the leaves as to make the plant undesirable from some points of view. The type plants, on the contrary, which are very much larger, have the heads large and regular and raised on long peduncles.

Ageratum Mexicanum, intermedium.

This variety, which is a bud-variety of second degree, that is, a sport from a sport (from the variety nanum), is intermediate. The plants are very floriferous. Their heads are also better than those of the type, and as they are borne upon longer peduncles, the plants are not only suitable for garden ornament but for cut flowers. The dimensions of this variety are intermediate between the last variety and the specific type.

Ageratum Mexicanum, variegatum.

This differs little from the type except by its leaves being variegated with yellowish-white on the margins. Its inflorescence is, however, a little more slender and its heads are smaller. In general, the plant is "leggy," weak.

Almond with variegated leaves.

Leaves bordered and made satin-like with white; vegetation delicate. It sometimes returns to the type.

Anemone Japonica, Honorine Jobert.

Very vigorous and very beautiful. This variety, of which the flower is white, is a bud-variety from the so-called A. hybrida or A. elegans, which was obtained in England by M. Gordon by crossing A. Japonica with A. vitifolia. The variety was produced some years ago at M. Jobert's, amateur at Verdun.

Apricot with variegated leaves.

Aralia trifoliata, Cookii.

This plant has its leaves, in general, simple, long, and narrow.

Arundo Donax, variegata argentea, and A. Donax, variegata aurea.

These varieties differ from the type by the leaves being bordered with white in the first, and with yellow in the second. They are much more delicate than the type.

Aspidistra elatior, variegata.

Aster bicolor.

This plant, which we believe not to be a distinct species but simply a dwarf form, very probably a bud-variety of A. versicolor, produced at the Museum in 1856, upon one of its stems, a vigorous bud which presents all the characters of A. versicolor except that it is a little smaller. This variety, to which we have given the varietal name Major, has preserved all its characters when multiplied by root-cuttings, and to-day is still one of the most beautiful perennial plants.

Azalea Indica, Dieudonné Spae.

Flowers salmon, margined with white. It is a sport from A. formosa, Ivery, which has rose flowers.

Azalea Indica, Beauté de l'Europe.

This variety has flowers white at the base, variegated with red. It is a sport from A. delicata, which has deep salmon flowers.

Azalea Indica, Criterion.

Flowers deep rose bordered with white. This is a sport from A. Iveriana, which has flowers white, striped with rose.

Azalea Indica, alba rosea.

Flowers rose, slightly bordered with white. A bud-variety from A. Iveriana.

Azalea Indica, exquisita grandiflora.

Flowers deep rose bordered with white. It is a bud-variety from A. alba perfecta, which has flowers white, very lightly striped with rose.

Buxus Balearica, cucullata.

This bud-variety of B. Balearica differs from its parent by its smaller leaves, which are very strongly convex, and rounded in the middle.

Buxus sempervirens, argentea.
Buxus sempervirens, aurea.
Buxus sempervirens, marginata.

All these varieties are distinguished from the type by their leaves being variegated or bordered with either white or yellow.

Camellia Japonica, Comte de Paris.

This variety, which has strongly striped rose-flesh-colored flowers, is a sport from the Duchesse d'Orléans, which bears white striped flowers. This variety is not only much more vigorous than its parent, but it has the merit of fully expanding its flowers, while the buds of the Duchesse d'Orléans almost always fall before opening.

Camellia Japonica, Montironi rosea.

This plant, whose flowers are entirely rose, is a sport from the Montironi, which has white, very lightly striped flowers.

Camellia Japonica, Giardino Franchetti.

Flowers deep rose, bordered with white. It is an offshoot from C. Targioni, which has white flowers lightly striped with rose.

Camellia Japonica, Comtesse Woronzoff.

This variety, which has delicate rose flowers, is a sport from C. centifolia alba, whose flowers are pure white.

Camellia Japonica, Giardino Schmitz.

Flowers delicate rose-color. It is a bud-variety from the Elisa Centurion, which bears very lightly rose-striped white flowers.

Camellia Japonica, Impératrice Eugénie.

Flowers rose-flesh-colored. A bud-variety from Montironi, whose flowers are very striped with rose.

Camellia Japonica, Paolina Armari.

Flowers deep rose. Bud-variety from Miss Abby Wilder, which has white, lightly rose-striped flowers.

Camellia Japonica, Princesse Aldrovandi.

Flowers rose, bordered with white. Sport from Teutonia, which bears flowers white, rose-striped.

Camellia Japonica, Bicolor de la Reine.

Flowers rose, bordered with white. It is a sport from de la Reine, whose flowers are white, lightly striped with rose.

Last year we saw upon a camellia with rose flowers, some branches bearing flowers completely white.

Cephalotaxus pedunculata, fastigiata.

This variety, which has been described and figured as being a species of Podocarpus (P. Koraiana), is an example of bud-variation. We had proof of this statement at the Museum in 1863. Having made cuttings from a certain number of branches of the so-called Podocarpus, one of them, instead of producing simple and scattered, strictly erect branches bearing scattered leaves, produced whorled, horizontal branches bearing distichous leaves. The variety fastigiata is to C. pedunculata what Taxus baccata, fastigiata, is to T. baccata.

Cereus Peruvianus, monstrosus.

Sometimes returns to the type.

Clematis bicolor or Sieboldii.

This plant, of which the flowers, violet inside, are almost double from the transformations of the stamens, is a sport from C. florida, which has single greenish-white flowers. We have several times had occasion to ascertain that such is the origin of this clematis.

The variety known as C. bicolor, flore pleno, which we sometimes call Atragene Americana, so remarkable for its enormous greenish-white flowers, is a direct sport from C. bicolor, consequently a bud-variety of the second degree from C. florida, a fact which we have been able to verify again this year. On a plant of C. bicolor, planted in the open air, there is developed, almost from the base, a branch which bore flowers entirely full, monstrous, yellowish-green, so that the two bud-varieties — C. bicolor and its variety flore pleno — were united upon the same individual.

Clematis, Helena monstrosa.

This plant is none other than C. Helena which, by bud-variation, is transformed and has become double flowered. This example is analogous to that which is produced by C. bicolor.

Cheiranthus Cheiri, variegata flore pleno.

Sport from the double-flowered yellow gillyflower of the walls.

Cherry. See page 170.

Cornus sanguinea, variegata.

Cornus Mas, variegata.

Cytisus Adami.

Whatever may be the origin of this plant, whether a hybrid, as is generally believed, or a peculiar form, we propose here to say nothing concerning it beyond a verification of its peculiarities. It develops very frequently and normally, so to speak, some branches of C. Laburnum and others belonging to C. purpureus. When we graft separately these two kinds of branches, these species remain invariable, although the grafts were taken from C. Adami.

Dactylis glomerata, variegata.

Echinocactus multiplex, cristata.

This variety, instead of having a regular, lengthened, melon-like stem, forms a thick mass which extends itself into little fan-shaped bunches, and instead of longitudinal furrows, large and deep, and separated by protuberances upon which are borne long, very rigid spines (about three-fourths to one and two-fifths inches); the variety has only very slight furrows or kind of folds disposed transversely to the direction of the fasciation, consequently in a contrary direction to those which are presented by the type, and upon the borders are spurs (about two-fifths inch long) disposed in stars. In a word, the variety is entirely different from its parent.

Elæagnus reflexa, variegata argentea and variegata aurea.

These two varieties differ from the type in having their leaves bordered, respectively, with white or yellow.

Elæagnus pungens, variegata.

Euonymus Japonica, argentea and aurea.

These, especially aurea, return sometimes to the type.

Euonymus Japonica, flavida.

This plant, which developed upon a type plant with green leaves in 1862, is distinguished by its leaves being bordered with yellowish-green, sometimes with nearly white. It is vigorous.

Euonymus Japonica, fasciata.

Very remarkable for its much fasciated branches. This variety appeared at the Museum in 1864, upon a typical E. Japonica.

Euonymus Japonica, calamistrata.

This sprung from the variety argentea, from which it differs in its more slender parts. Its leaves are smaller and crisped as if erose.

E. Japonica has also produced many other bud-varieties, which differ in variegation, or sometimes even by the form of the leaves. It is more than probable that the various varieties which have been introduced recently from Japan are bud-varieties.

Fagus sylvatica, fern-leaved.

This variety once presented the following peculiarity: Having grafted it upon the common beech, the branches developed from each side of the stem almost distichously. All those upon one side bore leaves similar to those of the common beech, whilst those upon the other side bore only laciniated leaves.

Ficus scandens, microphylla.

This variety, which we sometimes meet in commerce under the name of F. buxifolia, is a bud-variety which appeared in 1856 at the Botanic Garden of Orléans upon a plant of F. scandens grown in a greenhouse. Its leaves are very small, somewhat suborbicular and marked with brown. This variety is preserved in all its characters, both upon the original plant and in all the multiplications which have been made of it.

Fontanesia phyllireoides, variegata.

This very pretty variety appeared at the Museum in 1854. Since its appearing, this variety has not varied. Its branches, of a yellowish-green, are slender, and the leaves are deeply bordered with yellowish-white.

Fraxinus Americana, variegata.

Fraxinus excelsior, jaspidea.

This variety is distinguished by its bark being striped or slightly ribboned with yellow.

Fraxinus excelsior, variegata.

The common ash has produced several sports which are marked by the variegation of their leaves. This one has yellow and white disposed in bands and bordering the leaves, or sometimes in spots upon all parts of the blade, as upon the leaves of Aucuba, for example ; hence the various names, argentea, aurea, striata, maculata, aucubæfolia, etc.

Gardenia radicans, variegata.

In this instance the variation is two-fold. The leaves are bordered, and are also much narrower than in the type.

Gillyflower, called Savoyarde, with variegated leaves.

This is a sport from the double-flowered brown gillyflower.

Grape. See *Vine*.

Hedera. Variegated tree-ivy.

This sub-variety is a bud-variety from the so-called tree-ivy (*lierre en arbre*,) from which it varies only in the yellowish-white variegations of the leaves.

What we call tree-ivy is a common ivy, or one of its varieties, arrived at the full-grown state and which then fruits. The branches are large, short, cylindrical, and destitute of climbing roots. The leaves, instead of being lobed, are heart-shaped, more or less lengthened, sometimes very obtusely rounded. As there are several forms of creeping ivy, so there are several sub-varieties of the tree-ivy. They partake of the character of the varieties from which they come and are distinguished by the form and dimensions of the leaves, by the size of the branches, these characters all depending upon the vigor and appearance of the mother varieties. We obtain the tree-ivy either by cuttings or by grafting from adult branches, that is, branches which have been modified by fructification. They then branch and form very pretty bushes. Sometimes, especially near the ground or in badly aired places, branches arise supplied with climbing roots, bearing leaves more or less lobed, and which creep and take root as soon as they touch the ground. Here, in the case of the tree-ivy, is an instance of bud-variation due to the maturity of the individual.

Hibiscus Syriacus, flore pleno variegata.

This variety, whose leaves are variegated with yellowish-white, appeared in 1858 upon a plant with entirely green leaves.

Hibiscus Syriacus, variegata.

Remarkable in the variegation of its leaves. Its flowers are similar to those of the last. It is a variation directly from the type. It is not vigorous.

Hyacinth.

The double blue or Globe terrestre is a bud-variety from the double white or Sultan Achmet.

The double white with blue eye, or Sphæra Mundi, is a sport from the double white. The single red, called Acteur, cultivated for a very long time without varying, has produced by bud-variation at Hemstede, near Haarlem, a variety with double, imbricated red flowers. The hyacinth Ami du Cœur, with single blue flowers, also long cultivated without varying, has produced, from the same bulb, two flower stalks, one of which bore flowers dregs-of-wine color, while the other bore flowers of a delicate flesh-colored rose.

Hydrangea Hortensia.

This sterile plant is a sport from the form called H. Japonica, analogous to those which are produced upon Viburnum Keteleerii and V. Opulus.

Hydrangea Japonica, variegata.

Differs from the type only by its leaves being bordered with white.

Ilex Aquifolium, calamistrata variegata.

This variety is a sport from the I. calamistrata, which is a sport from the common holly.

Ilex Aquifolium, ferox aurea, and ferox argentea.

Bud-varieties from the variety ferox, from which they differ in the variegation of the leaves, yellow in the first, white in the second.

The very numerous varieties of common holly in cultivation are for the most part fixed bud-varieties.

Iris spectabilis.

This plant, so remarkable for its color, is a bud-variety from Iris Xiphium, from which, however, it is very different.

Juniperus communis, variegata.

Juniperus excelsa, variegata.

Juniperus Virginiana, variegata.

Juniperus Virginiana, monstrosa.

This variety, which arises from knaurs or burrs, is shown frequently upon the Virginian juniper (red cedar).

Lamium album, variegatum.

Laurocerasus vulgaris, angustifolia.

This plant, which for a long time has gone under the name of Hartogia Capensis, is a bud-variety, a fact which we have been able to ascertain several times. Its leaves are very straight, long, of a clear green, and more strongly toothed than those of the plant from which it comes. It is very constant. We have a record of its variation.

Laurocerasus vulgaris, variegata.

Laurocerasus Lusitanica, variegata.

Ligustrum Japonicum, variegatum.

The L. Japonicum appears to be subject to bud-variations, especially in the direction of dichroism. We have already produced from it several varieties distinct in the color or disposition of the variegations, the varieties receiving names according to their character. There is one which differs somewhat in the form of its leaves.

Ligustrum ovalifolium, aureum.

This variety, which is distinguished by having its leaves bordered or ribboned with yellow, was produced at the Museum in 1861. It comes from a branch which was developed spontaneously upon a type plant. It is unstable.

Ligustrum vulgare, variegatum.

This variety has leaves variegated with yellow. It occurs quite frequently in the wild state. We have found it several times in the woods. It is not stable.

Lilac, common, variegated.

Lilac, Persian, laciniate-leaved and white-flowered.

Although we are not able to state precisely when these two sports appeared, we have no doubt that they are bud-varieties, as the Persian lilac never gives seeds. The origin of the Persian lilac itself, even, is in much doubt.

Mamillaria nivea, dedalea.

This variety forms a compact mass whose folds and circumvolutions are disposed in a sort of labyrinth (whence *dedalea*), giving it a little the appearance of calves' pluck. The type from which this variety comes forms a melon-formed cylinder which is slightly swollen at the summit. It bears spines disposed in bundles and from about four-fifths inch to one inch and a fifth in length, rigid, very sharp, surrounded at the base by a series of smaller ones disposed in the form of a star. The variety, on the other hand, aside from its peculiar form, has no spines. It is invested upon all its parts with silky hairs, silvery and as soft as felt to the touch. The parent and offspring have nothing in common in their general form.

Mentha rotundifolia, variegata.

Molinia cœrulea, variegata.

Musa paradisiaca, vittata.

This is distinguished from the type by the white bands upon its leaves. The variegation is conspicuous upon the yellow plants. It often disappears with time, so that in the old plants we do not often find any trace of it.

Myrtle, common, variegated-leaved.

Frequently returns to the type.

Opuntia cylindrica, cristata.

In exterior characters this plant has nothing in common with the type, which forms a regular, cylindrical column. The variety, on the contrary, is made up of enlarged pieces placed against each other in different ways, much the same as those presented by the various species of opuntia which we call "Semelles du Pape."

Orange tree, Turkish.

This variety, which is a sport from a kind of Seville orange (probably from the Horned Seville orange), bears at times upon its various branches leaves narrow and irregular (as erose), variegated or rather satin-bordered, white, and, upon other branches, green leaves, large and strongly eared, as well as fruits which recall those of the Horned Seville orange.

Orontium Japonicum, variegatum.

Osmanthus Fortunei,[1] ovata.

This variety is unstable. After having preserved it for more than a year without varying, it has resumed in large part its primitive character, which is to have leaves long, exceedingly thorny

[1] The Olea ilicifolia of commerce. — CARRIÈRE.

and strongly nerved. Sometimes we find branches bearing leaves of different forms.

Osmanthus Aquifolius, variegatus.

Differs from the type by the yellowish-white variegations of the leaves.

O. Aquifolius, which we can consider as the representative in Japan of our common holly, appears, like the holly, to be very subject to bud-variation. We have no doubt that the varieties recently introduced from Japan originated in this manner.

Peach, carnation-flowered (Persica dianthiflora), and many-colored (P. versicolor).

These two varieties are sportive forms of P. rosæflora, of which the flowers are very deep red. Like this, the two varieties have double flowers, but of very different colors from those of their parent. The carnation-flowered has flowers of a flesh-colored rose. The many-colored, on the contrary, has white flowers striped or ribboned with brilliant rose. This last is very much more delicate than P. rosæflora or the carnation-flowered.

Peach, willow-leaved red Madeleine.

This variety, remarkable for the form of its leaves, which are very long and narrow, plane, glossy, very shortly toothed, is the result of a bud-variation from the variety designated by certain horticulturists as Madeleine de Courson (red Madeleine). It appears to us to have great resemblance to that very anciently known as the willow-leaved.

Peach, laciniate-leaved red Madeleine.

Leaves very strongly and coarsely toothed or laciniated.

Pears, variegated fruited.

The following pears have given by bud-variation variegated varieties: Duchesse d'Angoulême, Amanlis, Guénette or Madeleine, Saint-Germain, Bergamotte d'automne, Culotte de Suisse, etc. These bud-varieties are further remarkable in that the variegations extend to the branches and fruit, but not to the leaves, a character which distinguishes them from the next variety, which is likewise a bud-variety.

Pear, Amanlis, with yellow bark and leaves.

A very remarkable variety. We could almost say that it is pretty. It was developed upon a stem of Amanlis which presented nothing abnormal. It is very vigorous, and produces a most singular effect, with its parts all yellow except the bark, which is grayish-white. It has not yet fruited.

[One of the most marked cases of bud-variation which ever came under my notice was observed a few years ago upon a tree of Onondaga pear. One branch, so placed as to remove all possibility of its being a root-sprout or a graft, bore about a dozen pears which were intensely and uniformly russeted. They were so different in appearance from the pears upon the remainder of the tree that no one would suppose for a moment that they were the same variety. Even the Sheldon does not differ more widely from the Onondaga in appearance than did this singular sport.]

See page 174 for further notes on the pear.

Pelargonium zonale, Manglesii.

Distinguished from the species by its white variegated leaves, which are more deeply lobed, and by the weaker branches. It has, in its turn, produced several varieties by bud-variation.

The bud-varieties produced by P. zonale and P. inquinans (which are in reality only one) are very numerous. There are among them some varieties of such pronounced characters that, if we ignored their origin, we might consider them species.

Pelargonium hederæfolium, variegatum.

Phalaris arundinacea, picta and aurea.

These two varieties differ from the species in the variegation, which is produced by white in the first case and yellow in the second. They are exactly representative of the phenomenon which is observed in Arundo Donax, as well as in the sugar-cane.

Phlox decussata, white Croix de Saint-Louis.

This variety, of which the flowers are entirely white, appeared upon the variety Croix de Saint-Louis in 1863. The parent variety has white-striped rose flowers, and cross-form, whence its name.

Phragmites vulgaris, variegata.

Leaves bordered or margined with white.

Picea excelsa, tabulæformis.

This variety, which attains a height of scarcely more than a foot or two, and which spreads out horizontally so as to form a sort of carpet, is a most remarkable variation which resulted from a knaur or burr upon the stem of a very large spruce. It was produced in the park of Trianon at Versailles.

Pinus sylvestris, nana monstrosa.

Produced from a knaur from the stem of a large pine. It is dwarf and monstrous, remarkable for its long, unequal, crowded leaves, and by its slender, sometimes almost filiform, irregular branches, which are produced in such quantity that they sometimes completely conceal the branches and even the trunk.

Pinus sylvestris, nana compacta.

This variety is also the result of a knaur from a large pine. It attains but a foot or two in height. Its very short and numerous branches have already borne two crops of cones, some nearly ripe, small, though well formed, others much younger, still herbaceous.

Pittosporum Tobira, variegatum.

Populus Græca,[1] pendula.

We cannot say whence this variety came nor how it was obtained. It has been in cultivation very long. We have a singular experience to record concerning it. In 1858 we grafted fifteen plants of P. nivea with P. Græca, and, seven of the grafts growing, there was one which produced slender and drooping branches just like the variety pendula of P. Græca, of commerce. This phenomenon is one of the most curious which we know. The tree is planted in the nursery of the Museum at the side of one of its brothers, to which, physically, it bears almost no resemblance, although coming from the same parent plant.

[1] Undoubtedly our native large-toothed aspen, Populus grandidentata. — L. H. B.

Both are pistillate and are covered each year with catkins.

Potato.

Potatoes furnish many examples of bud-variation [" mixing in the hill "]. Many of our cultivated varieties are bud-varieties from the subterranean parts. Every year at digging time, if we wish to keep the varieties true, we are obliged to throw out those which, we say, are " degenerated." This so-called degeneracy constantly tends to remove the products from the starting-point, and has, then, the result of producing new varieties.

Modifications in potatoes may also occur in the manner of vegetation or growth of the underground parts. Such is the case in the variety called Pouse-debout [" tubers standing on end "]. This name was given the variety because the tubers, instead of lying horizontally, or nearly so, are placed upright, one against the other, much as small pieces of wood are arranged for the making of charcoal.

The Marjolin we consider nothing else than a peculiarity of vegetation. This is proved by the fact that its characters — not blossoming and maturing very early — are not constant. It has produced two other varieties by modifications of its underground parts. One variety is the Marjolin tardive [Late Marjolin], called also Marjolin de deuxième Saison, which is sometimes sold in the Paris markets for the Hollande jaune [Yellow Holland]. It is remarkable for the period of its growth, which is more prolonged than that of the type, and it is also covered each year with flowers, while its parent scarcely ever blossoms. The other variety has no resemblance to the Marjolin in form. It is round, and its sunken eyes give it exactly the appearance of the ordinary yellow potato. When we cultivated the Marjolin there was not a year when we did not obtain round ones, although we had planted long ones very true in appearance.

A very remarkable example of the modifications furnished by the ordinary yellow potato is the following: In a square planted exclusively with this variety, very true in appearance, we gathered a certain number of which the skin was more or less dark; some had yellow flesh, others white. Planted separately, these bud-varieties have given us potatoes round in form like the parent type, but among which there were found some entirely violet in both exterior and interior, and some had black flesh slightly marbled with white. This modification of color was not the only change. In some cases the quality was very much modified. Thus, instead of being nearly like the yellow potato, the flesh of these varieties was compact, neither good nor bad.

We give two other examples of bud-variation in potatoes, observed by us at the Museum in 1864: Half of a plat was planted with the smooth long yellow called Hollande, and half with the regular long red commonly called Vitelotte lisse. The first half yielded tubers similar to those which we had planted. The second half, on the contrary, produced tubers differing from the parent in color, being of a reddish-yellow, although the form remained about the same. The quality, also, did not vary, so that while we confounded them sometimes with the Hollande, we were able to distinguish them readily when cooked, as they remained whole, while the others fell to pieces.

On the end of a plat where we had planted fifty of the ordinary round yellow potato, one plant grew until late in the season and gave round potatoes of a deep red.

In this same year, 1864, in a square planted entirely to Chardon potato, we observed some plants exactly similar to the others in growth and appearance, but which differed entirely in the color of the flowers, being dull white, a little sulphur-colored, while those of Chardon are violet-rose or rose-violet. The tubers from these white-flowered plants differed from those of the type in being more round and regular and having less pronounced eyes. Aside from these variations, we have found among the Chardon both earlier and later varieties, and this in spite of the fact that we had planted only such tubers as appeared to be entirely true and which for a long time had produced no variations whatever. Here, as in the preceding cases, the modifications were from the tubers, seed not having been sown.

An instance similar to the above is reported by M. Joigneaux in the *Journal de la Ferme et des Maisons de Campagne:* Nine or ten years ago six beautiful tubers of a long, pale yellow potato were given us. In order to increase the number of hills we divided each tuber into three pieces. We planted them ourselves. The cultivating was also done by us. Some of the potatoes, a very small number, resembled the type, but the larger number were spherical, some yellow like the parent, others deep red.

All cultivators know that the smooth or even Vitelottes, whose eyes are few in number and scarcely perceptible, often produce tubers of various forms and with eyes so much sunken that it is almost impossible to peel them. Once we obtained a variety which, besides the many and deep eyes, produced, in considerable quantity, agglomerations which gave to the whole a monstrous form. They were veritable hydras. Although coming from the Vitelotte, which is a good potato, this variety was very acrid and bad.

All these examples show without doubt how a part of the varieties of potatoes are produced, and proves that they do not all come from seeds. We may convince ourselves of it when, having observed the growth of the plants, we mark the peculiar plants and gather their tubers separately. See, also, page 209.

The phenomena presented by potatoes prove that the cause of the appearing of new varieties is not always due, as we generally suppose, to crossing, as fecundation can act only upon the seeds. It is also very rarely that we practise crossing in potatoes, but we can number the varieties by the hundred. But it often happens that cuttings made from portions of the top of the plant produce varieties different from the parent. Moreover, the existence of numerous varieties of certain plants which we cultivate and which never produce seeds, proves beyond a doubt that there are causes aside from crossing which tend to the production of new varieties.

Prunus Mahaleb, variegata.

Aside from this variety, which is very pretty with its long and very slender branches and white-variegated leaves, P. Mahaleb has by bud-variation given several sub-varieties which are distinguished by the form of the leaves, and especially by the color of their variegations.

Almost all these varieties are more delicate than the type.

Rheum australe, variegatum.

Remarkable for the beautiful white variegation of the leaves.

Ribes nigrum, variegatum.

Leaves variegated with yellowish-white.

Ribes rubrum, variegatum.

Robinia hispida, arborea and macrophylla.

R. hispida, var. arborea of the gardens (R. macrophylla DC.), differs from the type by its greater vigor, its branches very much larger, the bark dark, glossy, and smooth, and by the thicker coriaceous leaves, which are glossy as if varnished. R. hispida, var. macrophylla of the gardens, is nearer the type than the last; it differs from it, however, by its greater vigor, and especially in its flowers, which, less abundant and a little more developed, are paler in color. Like the type, of which even the origin is doubtful, these varieties do not produce seeds.

The fact of the sportive production of the variety inermis upon R. hispida is wholly beyond doubt. Several times we have found the two sorts of twigs growing side by side upon the same branch. It is only necessary to multiply them separately in order to obtain distinct varieties.[1]

Robinia Pseudacacia, umbraculifera.

This plant, now so commonly used either for ornament, under the common name of Acacia boule, or as a dwarf shrub and considered as a forage plant, and called in consequence Acacia à faucher, comes, according to Turpin, from a knaur which appeared on the stem of a R. Pseudacacia. This fact does not surprise us. It shows us how important these singular excrescences may become.

Rose Eglanteria, punicea.

This differs from the ordinary yellow-flowered capucine rose (R. Eglanteria) in the color of the flowers, which is an orange-red. In many soils this variety returns more or less quickly to the type. It frequently happens that we may see even upon the same stem a red and a yellow flower. Sometimes we find a flower which presents these colors separately on opposite sides and of nearly equal extent, or some petals may be half red and half yellow. In general, the sport is less vigorous than the type, so that under the influ-

[1] Plants of normally thorny species are often found which bear no thorns. There is a so-called variety inermis of the honey-locust, Gleditschia triacanthos. Wild blackberries with smooth canes are occasionally found. In fact, most prickly or thorn-bearing plants vary much in these characters. — L. H. B.

ence of a slow modification we sometimes see the color gradually disappear, and at the end of a certain time we have a rose with completely yellow flowers in the place where we planted one with orange-red flowers.

For further notes on the rose, see pages 161 to 170.

Salix Babylonica, annularis.

Very remarkable for the form of its leaves. For a long time we have noticed it showing itself each year upon an old tree. The parts upon which it appeared, being generally weak, produced, instead of long, linear, plane leaves, those which were rolled up on the edges and distorted into rings. It is very constant. We have no examples of its reverting. It is much less vigorous than the type.

Sambucus nigra, variegata aurea and variegata argentea.

These two varieties differ from the species in the variegation, which is made by yellow in the first, white in the second. The second is much less vigorous than the type.

Sambucus nigra, monstrosa.

Analogous to Euonymus Japonica, fasciata. The flowers are also monstrous, and, up to this time, the seeds which they have produced have always been poor.

Solanum Dulcamara, variegatum.

Solanum tuberosum, variegatum.

Remarkable for its yellow-variegated stems and leaves. During the year previous to the appearing of this variety, its parent type presented no unusual characters. See Potato, page 201.

Spiræa Ulmaria, variegata.

Symphoricarpus vulgaris, variegata.

Symphytum officinale, variegatum.

Thuyopsis dolibrata, variegata.

This variety, of which the leaves are variegated with white, is remarkable for its vigor and its facility for forming heads when multiplied by cuttings.

Ulmus campestris, variegata, argentea, aurea picta, etc.

Variegated varieties of the common elm are numerous. They are distinguished both by the color and form of the variegations.

Viburnum Opulus, sterilis or Boule de neige.

Viburnum Opulus, sterilis variegatum.

Viburnum Keteleerii, macrocephalum.

Analogous to the sterile varieties of V. Opulus.

P

Viburnum Tinus, variegatum.

Viola Rothomagensis, pallida.

This variety, of which the two superior petals are pale lilac and spotted, while the three others are yellowish-white and lightly striped, was produced by bud-variation at the Museum.

We have said elsewhere that the phenomena of bud-variation could be divided into two classes, one group including those variations which appear abruptly, the other those which take place slowly. This violet falls under the latter group. In 1863 we received from the hills of Vernon a certain number of plants of V. Rothomagensis. Planted at the Museum, they preserved nearly all their characters except the villosity, which in large part disappeared the first year. During this year 1863 and the entire year 1864, they produced blue flowers abundantly. In the winter of 1864–65 all the plants perished except one. The remaining plant, instead of being covered with beautiful blue flowers as it had been the two preceding years, produced flowers almost white.[1]

Vine (Grape).

Bud-variation is comparatively common in the vine. [Frequent cases occur in the American

---

[1] This variation appears, after all, to have been an abrupt one. — L. H. B.

grapes.] It is well understood in this case, as the vine is one of the oldest of cultivated plants and it is multiplied almost always by cuttings; and as cuttings are made by millions each year a bud-variety soon becomes widely disseminated. It frequently happens that a shoot will produce grapes differing in form or color from those which are borne upon other shoots of the same vine. We may add that these variations nearly always present peculiar qualities also. We will cite examples.

Upon a plant of black-fruited Muscat grape we have observed for several years that some shoots produce white grapes.

The white seedless Corinth is a bud-variety from a variety which has much larger fruits, with seeds. This is a fact which we have several times observed upon bunches where some fruits were unusually developed and which contained seeds. The white Cornith is analogous to the Chasselas de Demoiselles.

A proprietor of large vineyards in the middle of France, the late Cazalis Allut, wrote some years ago as follows : —

"A stock of Téret produced with me, for several years, black grapes upon shoots of two of its arms, and gray grapes upon shoots of the other arms. A stock of Épiran gris, trained in cordon, is now about forty feet long. The first twenty feet produces constantly gray grapes and the remainder produces white ones. I have in an enclosure a stock of Epiran noir having several arms. The shoots of one of the arms give grapes almost twice as large as those on other parts of the vine."

Another viticulturist, M. Henri Bouschet of Montpellier, wrote very recently: —

"I had occasion for several years to see in my collection at Lot-et-Garonne, a plant of Prunella gris, which, sometimes upon one stem, sometimes upon two, bore black grapes, while the remainder of the vine bore gray ones. I have noticed for two years in my collection at Calmelte a most curious fact upon three grafts of a Spanish variety which came to me from the collection of Luxembourg, where it is called Parrel del Reyno de Lorca and which I have recognized as our Morastel noir. One of these three stocks has borne on one side, to my great surprise, black grapes similar to those of the Morastel, and upon the other side, constantly, white bunches having an appearance very different from an ordinary white Morastel, and presenting a foliage very different in size and form. This odd foliage appears to me to be identical with that of the Oyo de Rey de Morada, of which the bright yellowish-green leaves present very shallow rounded dentate lobes, while the leaves of the Morastel are deep green with deep divisions, the lobes acute, with teeth detached and terminating in a point."

A passage which we find in the *Parfait Vigneron* (edition of 1811) seems to confirm the opinions which we give concerning bud-variations in grapes: —

"A citizen of Vilmorin has observed a stock of Meunier to bear, upon some shoots, leaves and fruits of Maurillon précoce. A citizen of Jumilhac has seen likewise the Meunier become Maurillon."

Therefore the grape called Madeleine Juillet, Maurillon hâtif, etc., is only a sport from Meunier, a fact which shows, as we have said before, that the varieties produced by bud-variation may present qualities different from those presented by the plants from which they come.

Upon a plant of Pinot gris there appeared at the Museum in 1863 a shoot whose leaves were much variegated or striped with yellow. It produced a grape very similar to the variety from which it came. It appeared to be much less fertile, however.

In 1863 we observed two other very remarkable examples. One example concerns the Précoce Malingre, the other the variety designated by the name of Verjus. These examples present contrary results. Thus, while Précoce Malingre has long, oval, scattered fruits, and the bud-variety which appeared upon it had round fruits borne close together and larger than those of the type, the Verjus has slightly oblong or nearly spherical fruits and the bud-variety which was developed upon it had fruits long-oval and attenuated at both ends, and somewhat later than those of the type.

The Chasselas gros Coulard is a bud-variety which appears frequently upon the ordinary Chasselas. Its fruits are large and spherical. They often drop. It differs especially from the Chasselas by its stronger shoots with joints much closer together, and by its leaves being less lobed, a little longer and thicker, of a glossy green as if varnished. It differs also from the ordinary Chasselas in its temperament. It needs much heat and also shelter from the influence of the air. It generally succeeds well in forced culture.

The Chasselas de Demoiselles, remarkable for its fruits, which are scarcely larger than shot, is a bud-variety from the ordinary Chasselas. This phenomenon appears to be due to the partial abortion of the sexual organs and particularly of the anthers, whence results the lack of impregnation of the flowers and the consequent abortion of seeds. Propagated by cuttings, it preserves its characters. A variety with variegated leaves has appeared from the ordinary Chasselas.

Wigandia Caracassana, variegata.

Distinct by its leaves and even its branches being variegated with white. The variety appeared in 1862 upon a plant which, placed in the open air at the beginning of the season, presented no unusual characters.

III. FOCKE'S DISCUSSION OF THE CHARACTERISTICS OF CROSSES. (Translation of Chapter IV. of *Die Pflanzen-Mischlinge.*[1])

There is no absolute distinction between plants of a pure and those of a hybrid or mixed descent; there are therefore no signs by which one can, under all circumstances and with certainty, recognize the mongrel nature of a certain plant. Hybrids, nevertheless, often show a series of characteristics which indicate with greater or less accuracy their mixed descent. Certain rules can be made in regard to them, of which none, of course, is without exception.

I. THE SIMPLE PRIMARY CROSS (A × B).[2]

1. *All individuals formed by the crossing of two pure species or races are, if they have been*

[1] Focke uses the word *mischling* (derived from *mischen*, "to mix") in about the same sense in which we use the noun *cross;* *i.e.* it is a generic term for both cross-breeds and hybrids.

[2] In these formulas, the letters are used to designate the parents of any cross. In common with usage amongst botanists,

produced and grown under the same conditions, exactly like each other, as a rule, or they differ hardly more than specimens of one and the same species are apt to do.

This carefully stated proposition, founded upon experience, appears to be sufficiently justified by numerous experiments, but it is, nevertheless, subject to many exceptions. Some students of crosses have so limited its application that they dared only to assert the similarity of the specimens obtained from a capsule fertilized by the same plant. At all events, the rule proves itself to a certain degree trustworthy only in those cases in which the similarity of origin and condition of growth demanded by the terms of the rule are really present.

The question easiest to answer is just the one about which there has been the most violent discussion, namely, that relating to the stronger influence of the one or the other sex upon the offspring. The crosses of the two species or races A and B resemble each other whether A was male or female in the crossing. Experimenters, especially Kölreuter, Gärtner, Naudin, and Wichura, have not, on the whole, been able to find any

---

arbitrary signs are used in the text to designate the sex of each parent. The sign ♂ represents the male, or the parent which furnished the pollen; ♀ stands for the female or seed-bearing parent. — L. H. B.

difference between A ♀ × B ♂, and B ♀ × A ♂. More than one hundred years had passed since Kölreuter had proved the conformity of Nicotiana rustica ♀ × paniculata ♂, and N. paniculata ♀ × rustica ♂, when one of the acutest florists of our time, Timbal-Lagrave, was also astonished in the highest degree by a similar experience. All the rules and supposed experiences according to which the florists were to know, from the morphological characteristics of a hybrid, which of the progenitors had furnished the pollen for its formation, and which had borne the seed, are entirely groundless and foolish. Besides, it has been proved by many experiments, that in the vegetable kingdom, with regard to species, as a rule, the form-determining power of the male and female elements in the progeny is entirely equal.

As with all other rules touching the crossing of plants, this one of the similarity of the products of reciprocal crossings is not without its exceptions. It is a matter of course that an observed difference can be ascribed, with any probability, only to a stronger influence of the male or female elements, provided that the experiments are carried on in exactly the same manner, and if they always lead to the same result after repeated trials. So far, almost all the recorded experiments could be improved in this respect, for they are open to justifiable doubt. The following declarations of the differences in the products of reciprocal crossing seem worthy of notice.

a. The influence of the female element in Pelargonium fulgidum × grandiflorum, P. peltatum × zonale, Epilobium hirsutum × Tournefortii,[1] exceeds that of the male as regards general form. This influence is also shown more strongly in the colors of the flowers of several hybrids of Digitalis, in some also in the form of the corolla. In Nymphæa rubra × dentata, the seed-leaves resemble those of the female progenitors.

b. The female element shows, apparently, an overpowering influence in the power of withstanding cold in the Rhododendron (hybrids of R. arboreum), Lycium, and perhaps also in Crinum (hybrids of C. Capense).

c. The male element influences the general form especially in Papaver Caucasicum × somniferum, and Cypripedium barbatum × villosum (if constant?); it shows a stronger influence upon the colors of the flower in Petunia.

d. Gärtner says that he has sometimes observed differences in the fruitfulness and progeny of reciprocal hybrid forms, e.g. in Dianthus barbatus × superbus. The experiences of Gärtner should, however, hardly suffice to establish the uniformity of this occurrence.

The principal differences between A ♀ and B ♂

[1] The various examples cited in the text are fully explained in the body of Focke's work, *Die Pflanzen-Mischlinge*.

and B ♀ and A ♂ . have been observed by Kölreuter and Gärtner in some Digitalis hybrids. That these differences really show themselves each time and in the same manner, is by no means proved.

Much oftener, the departures from the regular uniformity of single specimens, observed among hybrids, are entirely independent of the influence of the species in the hybrid formation. Often important differences appear among the seedlings of the same cross which have been treated exactly alike. These differences show themselves in different ways: —

1. Single specimens of the cross may show but slight differences among themselves, especially in the color of the blossoms and similar characteristics, which are easily changed; compare, for example, the hybrids of Verbascum phœniceum, Salix Caprea × daphnoides.

2. The cross may appear in two different types, each of which represents a different combination of the characteristics of the progenitors. As a rule, one type more closely resembles the one, and the second the other progenitor; the numbers of the two types are often very unequal. Gärtner designated the rarer forms "exceptional types" (*Ausnahmetypus*). For examples, study Cistus, Dianthus, Geum, Œnothera, Lobelia, Verbascum Thapsus × nigrum, Nicotiana quadrivalis × Tabacum, var. macrophylla.

3. The cross may appear in several different types. Gärtner gives some examples of these, although in his cases it is probably a question of three known forms of one polymorphous union.

4. The cross may appear in a typical intermediate form, and a number of vacillating ones approaching one or the other parent, and among which no distinct type can be distinguished. Such is Medicago falcata × sativa, usually also Melandrium album × rubrum.

5. The cross may have from the beginning very many forms. The experiments which have been made leave it doubtful if in these cases one or more constant types, with a similar combination of characteristics, can be distinguished among the vacillating forms. Study Abutilon, hybrids of Pelargonium glaucum, P. radula × myrrhifolium, Passiflora, Hieracium, Nepenthes, Narcissus. Gärtner made the assertion that hybrids between two species are of similar form, whilst crosses of varieties are polymorphous. If, by varieties, is understood the unsettled garden forms or garden crosses, then the remark is justifiable; but if fixed races of pure descent are also included, then it is decidedly wrong. See " Cross-breeds and Hybrids " (section III., page 247).

Entirely different results are obtained by comparing hybrids which, although springing from the same species, were produced and grown in different places. Spontaneous hybrids are, as a rule, much more variable than those produced artificially, e.g. Verbascum Lychnitis × Thapsus and V. Lychnitis × nigrum. My hybrids between Digitalis purpurea and D. lutea resembled each other much when I had sown the seeds; on the other hand, very different forms arose when the seeds had accidentally sown themselves. It may be that in this case there was no real causative connection between the many forms and the manner of sowing; nevertheless it is certain that several growers have very often obtained different results in their crossings from the same species. The uniformity of all the products of the same crossing, which undoubtedly is the rule with the experiments of growers, appears in nature rather to be the exception than the rule. It remains to be ascertained what influence the unequal nourishment of the parent species, or of the hybrid seedlings, has upon the variability of the hybrids.

2. *The characteristics of the crosses may be different from the characteristics of the parent species. It is in size and luxuriance (see proposition 3), as well as in their sexual ability (see proposition 4), that they differ most from both parent species.*

The manner differs in which the characteristics of the parent species are united in the cross. Generally, a blending or mutual union takes place, but often in such a manner that in one respect one, and in another respect the other parent seems to appear. Sometimes, for example, the cross resembles one parent in the leaves, and the other parent in the flower. Sometimes there appears a variety of the cross, in which the characteristics are distributed in the reverse order. Some crosses resemble at first one species, and later the other parent species; as their leaves show in the spring the one and in the fall the other type (Cistus, Populus); or the colors of the flowers change during the blossoming (Melandrium album × rubrum, Epilobium roseum × montanum; compare also Lantana), or in the fall (Nicotiana rustica × Tabacum, Tropaeolum, Lobelia, etc.), also sometimes in different years (Bletia crispa × cinnabarina, Galium cinereum × verum). By the union of races (rarely in hybrids in the more restricted sense of the term), one finds, among other things, the characteristics of the parent species unmixed beside each other (compare Cucumis Melo, the thorniness of the Datura fruits, color of the flower in Rhododendron Rhodora × calendulaceum, R. Ponticum × flavum, Anagallis, Linaria vulgaris × purpurea, Calceolaria, Mimulus, Mirabilis). The colors of the flower often appear in an unexpected and unexplainable manner: the hybrids of Verbascum phoeniceum are very variable in the colors of the flowers, and in other respects quite uniform;

on the hybrids of Helianthemum have sometimes been found differently colored flowers on the same stalk, at the same time.

From the crossing of closely related races, especially varieties in color, there often appear plants which exactly or very closely resemble the parent types; compare Brassica Rapa, var., Linum, Pisum, Phaseolus; Anagallis, Atropa, Datura Stramonium, Salvia Horminum, etc. Usually the influence of the second parent race does not show itself till the second generation; and, in fact, in such a manner that a part of the seedlings return to that form, either entirely or only in certain respects. Only in Atropa, no return to the (slightly fixed) yellow form has been observed.

In some cases, the cross resembles one of the parent forms so much that it could be considered as only a slight variation of the same. Even in crosses between two considerably different species, the predominating influence of one parent species is sometimes shown in a striking degree. The hybrid of Dianthus Armeria × deltoides resembles D. deltoides much more than the other parent species; of D. Caryophyllus × Chinensis resembles D. Caryophyllus; of Melandrium rubrum × noctiflorum resembles M. rubrum; of Verbascum Blattaria × nigrum resembles V. nigrum; of Digitalis lutea × purpurea resembles D. lutea.

Sometimes even the primary hybrids show characteristics which are entirely different from either parent species; especially is this the case, amongst other things, in the colors of the flowers. The most curious is the regularly blue-flowering hybrids of the white Datura ferox with the equally white D. lævis and D. Stramonium, var. Bertolonii. There are many examples of unexpected coloring of the blossoms of hybrids from species of colored flowers, while the crosses by no means always show the shades of color which would be obtained by a mixture of the parental pigments. Noticeable instances are shown, *e.g.*, by Clematis recta × integrifolia, Aquilegia atropurpurea × Canadensis (and others), Nicotiana suaveolens × glutinosa, Verbascum pulverulentum × thapsiforme, hybrids of V. phœniceum, Anemone patens × vernalis, Begonia Dregei × Sutherlandi (and others). In the crosses of races, *e.g.*, of Papaver somniferum and Datura Stramonium, many characteristics appear which belong not to the parent forms, but to other races of the same species. Nicotiana rustica × paniculata sometimes shows the colors of the blossoms of N. Texana, a foreign sub-species of N. rustica. Other characteristics which the hybrids show in a greater degree than the parent forms, are, *e.g.*. the greater stickiness of some hybrids of Nicotiana (rustica × paniculata).

the apparently greater wealth of honey in N. rustica × paniculata, the stronger nauseous odor of the hybrids of Melandrium viscosum, the supposed increase in the quantity of quinine (?) in hybrids of Cinchona (according to Kuntze).

In later generations of hybrid growth, deviations from the characteristics of the parent species are much oftener observed.

3. *Crosses of different races and species are distinguished from plants of a pure race, as a rule, by the power of vegetation.* Hybrids *between very different species are often very weak, especially when young, so that it is difficult to successfully raise the seedlings. On the other hand, crosses of more closely related species and races are, as a rule, uncommonly luxuriant and strong; they are distinguished mostly by size, rapidity of growth, early flowering, abundance of flowers, longer life, stronger reproductive power, unusual size of some special organs, and like characteristics.*

For a closer confirmation of this proposition, it will be to the purpose to refer to some examples. Delicate seedlings are mentioned, e.g., in Nymphaea alba crossed with foreign species, Hibiscus, Rhododendron Rhodora with other species, R. Sinense with Eurhododendron, Convolvulus, polyphyllous Salix hybrids, Crinum, Narcissus. The experience that seedlings of hybrid-fertilized seeds are delicate, is frequent. A dwarfish growth has rarely been observed in hybrids, although there are some instances of it. Large growth is, on the other hand, much more common, *e.g.*, Lycium Datura, Isoloma, Mirabilis. Usually the hybrids exceed in height both parent species, or at least their medium height; compare, *e.g.*, many hybrids of Nicotiana, Verbascum, Digitalis. The vegetation sometimes takes place exceedingly fast. Klotzsch emphasizes the rapid growth of his hybrids of Ulmus, Alnus, Quercus, and Pinus. The flowering time often comes earlier than in the parent species, *e.g.*, in Papaver dubium × somniferum, some Dianthus hybrids, Rhododendron arboreum × Catawbiense, Lycium, Nicotiana rustica × paniculata, Digitalis, Wichura's six-fold Salix hybrid, Gladiolas, Hippeastrum vittatum × Reginae, etc., but especially in many hybrids of Verbascum. On the other hand, there are, no doubt, also single hybrids which blossom only after a long period, or not at all, *e.g.*, in the genera Cereus and Rhododendron. Only one example of earlier maturity of seeds, independent of an earlier maturing of the blossoms, is known to me, namely, in Nuphar. Very often and very commonly an extraordinary abundance of flowers has been observed in hybrids; compare, *e.g.*, Capsella, Helianthemum, Tropaeolum, Passiflora, Begonia, Rhododendron, Nicotiana (rustica × paniculata, glutinosa × Tabacum, and others), Verbascum,

Digitalis, many Gesneraceæ, Mirabilis, Cypripedium. The size of the blossoms is often increased in hybrids; in a cross of two species with different sized flowers it is not rare that the flowers of the hybrid attain the size of those of the larger-flowered parent, or almost that size. Dianthus arenarius × superbus, Rubus cæsius × Bellardii, hybrids of Rosa Gallica, Begonia Boliviensis, Isoloma Tydæum, give examples of uncommonly large flowers.

A strong vegetative reproductive power is very common among hybrids; compare, *e.g.*, Nymphæa, hybrids of Rubus cæsius, Nicotiana suaveolens × Tabacum, var. latissima, Linaria striata × vulgaris, Potamogeton. A longer life is especially noticeable in some hybrids of Nicotiana and Digitalis. A greater power of resistance against cold is also noticeable in Nicotiana suaveolens × Tabacum, var. latissima, while Salix viminalis × purpurea is said to be more sensitive to frost than either of the parent species.

These facts indicate partly a certain loss of vigor which is inherent to the hybrids on account of their abnormal descent, and partly, on the contrary, an exceptional vegetative power. This latter fact, which occurs much oftener than the former, has only lately been elucidated to any extent. The important experiments of Knight, Lecoq, and others, had been known for some time, but only through the careful researches of Charles

Darwin has the favorable influence of a cross between different individuals and races of one and the same species been clearly shown. The strengthening of the vegetative power in some hybrids is evidently a universal experience which needs no special explanation, on account of the peculiar circumstances of the formation of the hybrids. It was formerly thought that the diminished sexual fruitfulness is compensated by a greater vegetative luxuriance, a statement the untenableness of which, as Gärtner showed, is most plainly shown by the fact that many of the most fruitful crosses (Datura, Mirabilis) are also distinguished by an enormous growth.

4. *Hybrids of different species often form in their anthers a smaller number of normal pollen grains, and in their fruits a smaller number of normal seeds, than plants of a pure descent; sometimes they produce neither pollen nor seeds. In crosses of nearly related races, this weakening of the sexual organs does not occur as a rule. The blossoms of sterile or slightly fruitful hybrids usually remain fresh for a long time.*

No characteristic of hybrids has received more attention than the diminution of the sexual power which has been observed in them. Even Kölreuter believed that this characteristic permitted the drawing of a sharp line between species and varieties. The same thought has prevailed amongst botanists to a great extent since then, and even in very recent times Naudin, Decaisne, and Caspary have defended the ideas of Kölreuter in a more or less modified form. Knight, Klotzsch, and formerly also Gordon, considered the pollen of hybrids to be entirely impotent, a view which was even then contradicted by the accurate experiments of Kölreuter. It has often been wrongly declared that Kölreuter had himself spread the doctrine of the total sterility of hybrids; this assertion is to be explained only by ignorance or by a misunderstanding of the Latin text. Kölreuter, in fact, does not speak of sterility, but of lessened fruitfulness, as being a common characteristic of hybrids.

The fruitfulness of hybrids is considerably different, according to the individual genera. For instance, the hybrids of Papaver, Viola, Verbascum, and Digitalis show but little fruitfulness; the hybrids of Anemone, Nicotiana, Mentha, Crinum, the Cucurbitaceæ, and Passiflora are much oftener fruitful, while in Aquilegia, Dianthus, Pelargonium, Geum, Epilobium, Fuchsia, Cotyledon, Begonia, Cirsium, Erica, Rhododendron, Calceolaria, Quercus, Salix, Gladiolus, Cypripedium, Hippeastrum, the Gesneraceæ, and Orchidæ, the fruitful hybrids are commoner than the barren ones. In the genera Vitis, Prunus, Fragaria, and Pyrus, we use the crosses of closely related species as fruit plants; in Cereus, hybrids of even widely different species show undiminished fruitfulness.

The sterility of hybrids is sometimes shown by their exhibiting no inclination to blossom, a characteristic which has been observed particularly in some hybrids of Rhododendron, Epilobium, Cereus, and Hymenocallis. These are, however, rare exceptions, for as a rule hybrids bloom earlier and more profusely than the pure species (see page 226).

In hybrids which have flowers of only one sex, the staminate blossoms often fall off while they are yet buds, as in Cucurbitaceæ and Begonias (hybrids of B. Froebeli). Sometimes the anthers are arrested in their growth and form hermaphrodite flowers, as has been observed in some hybrids of Pelargonium and Digitalis (D. lutea × purpurea form tubiflora Lindl.). The common result of the production of hybrids is a different formation in the pollen grains in the hybrids from that of the parents. Often the anthers of the hybrids are dead and contain no pollen, or they are small and do not open at all. Such deficiency of pollen can be observed, for example, in Rubus Idaeus × odoratus, Ribes aureum × sanguineum, Alopecurus geniculatus × pratensis. In other cases, the pollen dust consists of small powdery grains of irregular form and size, which do not swell when moistened, and among which are usually found a few well-formed pollen cells which are capable of germination. Often the number of normal pollen grains is greater, and comprises ten or twenty per cent, or more, of the whole number. There are often found, in a greater or less degree, large angular grains capable of swelling, as well as well-formed ones, by the side of those dwarfed or stunted. Among crosses of closely related species, as Melandrium album × rubrum, there are usually found only few irregularities in the form of the pollen grains. In a hybrid Sinningia, the pollen of the second year of flowering was better than that of the first.

In hybrids of undoubted different species, a normal formation of the pollen is seldom seen. The statements on this subject require, for the most part, corroboration, nevertheless I refer to Nymphaea Lotus × rubra, Begonia rubrovenia × xanthina, Isoloma Tydaeum × sciadocalyx, Salix purpurea × repens; almost perfectly formed pollen grains were found in Salix aurita × Caprea, and S. viminalis × repens.

On the other hand, it is still more rare that a deficiency of pollen is found in an evident cross of races. Perhaps it could be found oftener if one sought for it. The only certain example of which I know is an Anagallis cross by myself. Whether Raphanus sativus and R. Raphanistrum are to be considered as species or races is doubtful. Nevertheless there are some crosses of very closely related species which appear to be entirely sterile, as, for example, Capsella rubella × Bursa-pastoris, Viola alba × scotophylla, Papaver dubium × Rhœas.

The sexual capabilities of the female organs are, as a rule, not so much weakened in hybrids as the male. Nevertheless they are greatly diminished. Many hybrids never produce fruit. Even after many experiments, one must not make definite assertions about the absolute sterility of a hybrid: in Rubus cæsius × Idæus, for example, one can see several thousand blossoms remain sterile, and nevertheless, now and then, fruit is produced. Compare, further, Digitalis lutea × purpurea, Lobelia fulgens × syphilitica, Crinum Capense × scabrum. A morphologically distinguishable defect of the ovule of hybrids has seldom been referred to so far, although it has been observed in Cistus, by Bornet. If one wishes to obtain a definite judgment on the female creative power in hybrids, he must fertilize the ovules with pollen of the parent species, which, as a rule, develops more perfect fruit than the pollen of hybrids which has been weakened in its generative power. In some cases, hybrids whose pollen shows but slight potency produce normal fruit with pollen from the parent, as in Luffa.

Some hybrids drop their entire blossoms unwilted, with the calyx and flower stalk intact, e.g., Ribes, Nicotiana rustica × paniculata, and other hybrids of Nicotiana.

As a rule, the corolla wilts, after a longer period, in a normal manner, or is thrown off as in the parent species; but no setting of fruit thus takes place, or only a little of very poor character. Sometimes the fruit is well formed externally, but contains no seed. In many cases hybrids set fruit, but to a less extent and with fewer seeds than the parent species. Even in crosses of closely related species, the number of seeds seems to be smaller than in the parent species; so, for example, according to Gärtner, in Melandrium album × rubrum, Lobelia cardinalis × fulgens, and even in undoubted crosses of races of Verbascum.

Hybrids of essentially different races rarely show an undiminished fruitfulness, although no noticeable diminution has been proved in Brassica Napus × oleracea, Dianthus Chinensis × plumarius, var. Sibiricus, Pelargonium pinnatum × hirsutum, Abutilon, Medicago, a few Cereuses and Begonias, Hieracium aurantiacum × echioides, Nicotiana alata × Langsdorffii, a few hybrids of Erica, Calceolaria, Isoloma, Veronica, and several Orchidæ. Fruits and seeds in abundance are also found in many other garden hybrids, and in many wild ones, as in Roses, Epilobiums, Fuchsias, Cirsiums, Hieraciums, Willows, of Lobelia Lowii, etc. In these cases, however, one cannot exactly ascertain if the plants are primary hybrids, or, which is much more probable, if they belong to later generations or arose through derivative hybridization (*Rückkreuzungen*).

In order to set seeds, or at least to produce a vigorous progeny, some hybrids require to be fertilized by other individuals, even though they are themselves hybrids; compare, for example, hybrids of Cistus, Begonia, Gladiolus, and Hippeastrum. In some hybrids, only the first flowers produce seeds, as Aquilegia, Dianthus, Silene, Lavatera Thuringiaca × Pseudolbia, Rubus foliosus × Sprengelii; in other cases, the first flowers are regularly sterile, while the later ones are often fruitful, as in Datura, Nicotiana rustica × paniculata, N. rustica × quadrivalvis, Mirabilis. In longer-lived plants, often all the flowers of the first years are sterile, while later, when the plant has reached a certain age, a few fruits are formed; this has been noticed, for example, in Rubus Idaeus × caesius, R. Bellardii × caesius, Calceolaria integrifolia × plantaginea, Crinum Capense × scabrum.

Although, as a rule, the female creative power in hybrids is less weakened than the male, still there are some cases in which the reverse is true; compare Nymphaea Lotus × rubra, Ciconium × Dibrachya in the genus Pelargonium,

Lobelia fulgens × syphilitica, Verbascum thapsiforme × nigrum, Narcissus montanus, etc; these are probably, for the most part, only accidental occurrences.

The longer duration of the flowers (especially the pollinized ones) on many sterile hybrids, is an occurrence which is analogous to the longer duration of unfertilized or incompletely fertilized flowers. Often in sterile hybrids, especially after dusting with the pollen of the parent or a related species, the fruits swell more or less without perfect seeds' being formed in them. Externally well-formed but seedless fruits are found in Cacti, Passifloras, Cucurbits, and Orchids. Gärtner has studied this characteristic, which is of no special use or value in the culture of hybrids, very carefully; however, it offers an important proof of the truth of the statement that the development of the outside coats of the fruits takes place in a normal manner on account of the irritation which the germinating pollen produces, but that it is nevertheless independent of the fertilization of the ovule, and the development of the embryo and of the seed.

One can, in general, make the statement that hybrids of closely related races are more fruitful on the average than those of considerably different species. One can also consider, as a rule, as has been shown above, that closely related species form hybrids among themselves more easily than those considerably different. Both rules are true only to a certain extent. If one should infer from these that hybrids are more fruitful the easier they are formed, then he would go far wrong. There is no definite relation between ease of formation and fruitfulness of crosses.

From a teleological point of view, we formerly saw in the sterility of hybrids a means of keeping "species" separate. What purpose this separation was to serve was not explained, unless it was for the convenience of the systematist. Now, on the contrary, we ask if the formation and separation of species does not really depend upon the fruitfulness of the crosses between the distinctly marked races of the parent types. The noticeable resemblance between illegitimate and hybrid progeny gives us no standpoint for further investigation of the cause of unfruitfulness. More light may be given by the fact that in the hybrid pteridophytes and mosses the formation of sexless spores is just as much wanting as is the formation of pollen grains in hybrid phanerogams. The obstacle to the regular propagation of hybrids seems to lie in the development of certain cells which have the power to maintain the type of the parent form, it being immaterial if these cells have sexual functions or not. In any case, more facts must be gathered to justify the adoption or presentation of a principle of such scope. This view of the situation can even now be considered as a hypothesis which certainly as yet offers no explanation of the limitations of species, but it leads the way to a final solution, because it brings a long list of different but plainly analogous phenomena as facts in the animal and vegetable kingdoms under one common point of view.

5. *Malformations and curious forms are much more common, especially in the flower parts of hybrids, than in individuals of a pure descent.*

Compare Papaver, Dianthus, Pelargonium, Nicotiana, Digitalis. Double flowers appear to be formed especially easily in hybrids.

II. THE PROGENY OF CROSSES.

Hybrids are more easily and completely fertilized by the pollen of the parent forms than by their own. Exceptions to this rule are hardly known (although compare Hieracium echioides × aurantiacum), although no large number of experiments have been made in this direction. By their own pollen is to be understood the pollen of hybrids of the same cross, as well as that of the same individual. When hybrids grow in the vicinity of parent forms, they must naturally often be fertilized by them. In the progeny there will be, therefore, a number of forms between the primary hybrids and the parent species. In sowing the seeds of hybrids, one cannot always determine if fertilization from the parent species could have taken place or not. The general statement that the progeny of a hybrid has shown itself to be very variable is therefore of little weight or worth. Sometimes a hybrid is more easily fertilized by a third species than by its own pollen. Compare, for example, Nicotiana rustica × paniculata, and Linaria purpurea × genistæfolia.

1. *Progeny of Crosses with their own Pollen.*

$(A \times B) \female \times (A \times B) \male$.

a. If one protects the fruitful hybrids from the influence of the parent forms or other related species, then he obtains hybrids of the second generation. It seems to me that the progeny of hybrids appears or acts very differently according to the length of their life. In long-lived plants, the mingling and mutual blending of the two types which have been joined in the hybrid often appears to be more complete, so that the progeny also inherits the characteristic of the new intermediate form or type in an equal or uniform manner.

The progenies of one- or two-year hybrids are, as a rule, very different and varied in form; compare Pisum, Phaseolus, Lactuca, Tragopogon,

Datura, Nicotiana alata × Langsdorffii, etc. Exceptions are found in Brassica, Œnothera, Nicotiana rustica × paniculata, Verbascum Austriacum × nigrum.

The progenies of hybrids of several generations (*mehrjähriger*) are generally similar, although the cases in which the intermediate type shows itself to be constant appear to be much more frequent. Some hybrids of Aquilegia, Dianthus, Lavatera. Geum, Cereus, Begonia, Cirsium, Hieracium, Primula, Linaria, Veronica, Lamium, and Hippeastrum appear to come very true to seed.

The progenies of shrubs and trees are, in the majority of cases, very constant or invariable; compare Æsculus, Amygdalus, Prunus, Erica, Quercus, Salix. Also many hybrids of Fuchsia and Calceolaria are said to be constant. The Rhododendron hybrids are partly true to seed and partly variable. The progeny of the crosses of Vitis, Pyrus, and Crataegus, on the other hand, seem to be very variable.

b. The several forms in which some primary hybrids appear seem to be unsettled in the progeny. In Dianthus, according to Gärtner, the "exception types," when sown, mostly return to the normal mongrel form. The various primary forms of the hybrids of Hieracium, Mendel found to be true to seed.

c. C. F. von Gärtner and other botanists have

made the assertion that the progeny of hybrids becomes, from generation to generation, weaker and less fruitful. It is certain that their growth, which was at first increased, gradually decreases when they fertilize themselves. Gärtner's experiments, however, were made on a very small scale, so that his hybrids were influenced not only by close in-breeding, but also by the various circumstances which so often result in the loss of garden plants cultivated only in small numbers. Even Gärtner noticed exceptions, as in Aquilegia, Dianthus barbatus × Chinensis, D. Armeria × deltoides. Crosses of closely related species evidently can be continually propagated or kept up with ease; compare Brassica, Melandrium, Medicago, Petunia. Many gardeners assert with much confidence that many hybrids can be propagated very well for several generations by means of seeds; compare Erica, Lychnis, Primula Auricula × hirsuta, Datura. Many observations of wild plants seem to confirm this view. The principle has also been laid down that the fruitfulness of hybrids increases again in later generations. It does not, however, appear that this rule can have a very broad application. It is much more probable that single fruitful specimens arise among hybrids, which can easily reproduce themselves under favorable external conditions by inheriting this peculiarity. Fruitful descendants of hybrids are probably sometimes the product of derivative hybridization.

d. Complete reversions to the parent forms without the aid of pollen from parent forms arise only in crosses of closely related races. Even in such crosses, true reversions only seldom take place, *e.g.*, Phaseolus.

e. From the variable progeny of fruitful crosses a few principal types often arise after a few — perhaps three or four — generations. If one protects these new types from crossing, they tend to become constant or fixed. Scientific trials or experiments which confirm this statement have been made only to a small extent, especially by Lecoq in Mirabilis, by Gordon in Linaria and especially in Datura. These gardeners have produced many new races by the crossing of related species and well-fixed races. Also many wild, fixed, intermediate forms may have arisen in this manner; compare Brassica, Lychnis, Zinnia, Primula, Petunia, Nicotiana commutata, Pentstemon, Mentha, Lamium. The new types of the descendants of crosses frequently differ in some characteristic from both parent forms. My Nicotiana rustica × paniculata had in the second and third generations, on the whole, much smaller leaves than either of the parent forms.

f. The sterility and inconstancy of the progeny of hybrids have often led botanists to conclusions which are not confirmed by experience. It is entirely wrong, as can be seen by the facts which have been stated, to assert that all crosses would necessarily soon be lost on account of these characteristics which have been promiscuously ascribed to them. The unsettled forms arising from crosses are the plastic material out of which not only gardeners form their new varieties, but which material is biologically the more valuable as it furnishes new species in the household of nature.

2. *Derivative Hybridization of Crosses with the Parent Forms.*

$$(A♀ \times B♂)♀ \times A♂, \ (A♀ \times B♂)♀ \times B♂, \ A♀ \times (A \times B)♂.$$

As long as one laid much stress upon the male or female influence which one or the other parent species may have had upon the hybrid, a difference was carefully made between the advancing hybrid forms, or those which more closely resembled the male parent, and the degenerating hybrid forms, or those which more closely resembled the female parent. But these differences are, according to experiments that have been made, of very subordinate importance, or, perhaps, of none at all.

By treating hybrids with parental pollen, one obtains, as a rule, a rather varied progeny. The intermediate form between the hybrid and respective parent is apt to be more numerous and more fruitful. Besides this, there are formed a less number of individuals, some of which resemble the hybrid, and some the parent species. Both are apt to be but slightly fruitful.

The three-fourths hybrids, (A × B) ♀ × A ♂, are often quite fruitful with their own pollen and appear to give races true to seed easier than the original hybrid; compare Ægilops speltæformis. Gärtner observed frequently that in later generations the pollen became more regular and the fruitfulness greater, as in Dianthus (Chinensis barbatus) × barbatus, and also in other three-fourths hybrids of Dianthus, Lavatera, and Nicotiana.

If one treats the three-fourths hybrid (A × B) ♀ × A ♂ again with pollen from A, then he obtains a seven-eighths hybrid, or the third hybridized generation, which, as a rule, is very much like the parent which furnished the seven-eighths part, but it is still apt to show marked differences in form and fruitfulness in some individuals. The last traces of the one original parent species disappears mostly in the fourth, fifth, or even sixth hybridized generation.

Kölreuter and Gärtner have completed the transition of one parent species into the other in many cases. They found that for a complete change, three to six generations were necessary — as a rule, four to five. Evidently the greater or less duration of the change depends more or less upon surrounding circumstances. Gordon found that Melandrium album × rubrum was like the parent species in the second generation, when fertilized with its own pollen, while Gärtner found three to four generations necessary to bring the one into the other by means of parental pollen.

As a rule, the products of the fertilization of a parent species with pollen from a hybrid, as A♀ × (A × B)♂, are similar to those of the opposite cross; nevertheless the statements of observers agree that the variety of forms is apt to be greater when one uses the hybrid as the male element; compare Dianthus and Salix.

There appears, in the products of derivative hybrids of crosses, as among the direct progeny, new characteristics, which are lacking in the parent forms, but are for the most part found in related races or species.

3. *Hybrids of Several Species.*

a. Triple Hybrids.

In the first years of his experience, Kölreuter succeeded in uniting three entirely different Nicotiana species into one hybrid form. The simplest formulas according to which such a union could take place are: $(A \times B) ♀ \times C ♂$, $C ♀ \times (A \times B) ♂$, and $(A \times B) ♀ \times (A \times C) ♂$. In the genera Dianthus, Pelargonium, Begonia, Rhododendron, Nicotiana, Achimenes, Calceolaria, Salix, Hippeastrum, Gladiolus, and a few others, there has been made a number of such unions without any particular difficulty. One must nevertheless determine if he unites three essentially different species, or if two of the factors, or even all three are only closely related to each other. There are similar but evidently different species which, in crossings among themselves, behave almost like races of the same species, as for example: —

Melandrium album and rubrum.
Vitis vinifera, cordifolia, aestivalis and Labrusca.
Lobelia fulgens, splendens, and cardinalis.
Rhododendron Ponticum, arboreum and Catawbiense.
R. flavum, viscosum, nudiflorum, and calendulaceum.
Berberis Aquifolium, and the most closely related species.

Hybrids between the crosses of two species of these groups with the third species of the same genus, can no more be called true triple hybrids than crosses of species belonging to some smaller or narrower group of Vitis, Lobelia, and Rhododendron. True triple hybrids which have been formed from three essentially different species are apt to be much varied in form, especially if the male parent species was a hybrid. On the other hand, in those unions which are most easily formed and are made by the formula (A × B) ♀ × C ♂, the type of C is apt to predominate strongly, as, for instance, Nicotiana (rustica × paniculata) ♀ × Longsdorffii ♂, Achimenes (grandiflora × candida) ♀ × longiflora ♂, and other Gesneraceæ.

The hybrids of Erica are said to produce just as uniform a progeny as the pure species. Several Salix hybrids have acted in the same manner.

For gardeners, therefore, the triple hybrids in some genera (as in Pelargonium, Begonia, Rhododendron, Achimenes, Isoloma, Cypripedium, Gladiolus) are very valuable. If they produce seeds, their progeny is very variable.

b. Hybrids of Four to Six Species.

If one does not count the crossings of very nearly related species (as Vitis, Rhododendron, etc.), these hybrids of four or more parent forms are somewhat rare. We know them especially in the genera Dianthus, Pelargonium, Begonia, Rhododendron, Nicotiana, Salix, Hippeastrum, Gladiolus. The artificial union of different species in a single hybrid form has been carried farthest by Wichura, who united six Salix species.

c. Crosses of Plants Grown Together.

In some genera, as Pelargonium, Fuchsia, Begonia, Rosa, Erica, Rhododendron, Achimenes, Calceolaria, Gladiolus, Hippeastrum, gardeners have crossed species and hybrids in the most manifold manner, intentionally and unintentionally, and have used the most promising forms obtained for further propagation. The progeny of this complex crossing is naturally almost always very variable. There appear, however, to be exceptions to this rule; Sweet plainly asserts that one always obtains the same cross from the crossing of some complex Pelargonium hybrids. Such constant complicated hybrids are, according to him, P. (hyb.) involucratum × (hyb.) ignescens and P. (hyb.) Mostynae × (hyb.) ignescens. That the Erica and some Salix hybrids produce a uniform progeny has already been mentioned.

III. CROSS-BREEDS AND HYBRIDS.

According to usage, we designate unions of two different varieties of one species as cross-breeds, unions of two different species as hybrids. It is necessary, on account of the indefiniteness of the term " variety," to remember that only varieties true to seed, or races and sub-species, can bequeath their characteristics with any degree of certainty;

inconstant species, which are so often designated as varieties, are not considered in the theory of hybridization.

Many writers have taken great pains to find a difference between cross-breeds and hybrids; they held firmly to the hope that by means of trials in crossing a boundary between species and sub-species could be formed. Gärtner, who expresses himself plainly in several parts of his work that the appearance of crosses clearly proves the specific differences of relationships of the parent forms, becomes very reticent as soon as he attempts, on pages 574–582, connectedly to unfold the principles of "variety hybrids." Herbert and Naudin have formed the opinion, after their many experiments, that it is impossible to draw the line between cross-breeds and hybrids; but, nevertheless, later botanists have again tried to find precise differences between them.

The following propositions have been made:—

1. The pollen of cross-breeds is normal: hybrids have a greater or less number of imperfectly formed grains in their pollen.

2. The fruitfulness of cross-breeds is normal: that of hybrids plainly diminished.

3. Hybrids of two species with differently colored blossoms produce flowers of mixed or uniformly modified colors: plants with irregular, mottled flowers have always been produced by

the crossing of varieties. It is the same with the coloring, marking, covering of the fruits, and other characteristics.

4. Cross-breeds have a strong inclination to return to the parent form in later generations.

These four propositions are in the main correct, but they offer little help, in a case of doubt, to a right decision as to specific merits. The cross of the red and white Anagallis arvensis would have to be considered as a hybrid on account of its pollen, and as a cross-breed on account of the appearance of flowers of two colors. In Datura, crosses, which in other respects are plainly characterized as hybrids, easily show complete returns to the parent forms. Hybrids whose fruitfulness appears to be in no way diminished have already been mentioned (page 229). One can, consequently, make the rule, that crosses of closely related races are apt to show the characteristics ascribed to cross-breeds, but it is impossible by that means to establish any sharp line between race crosses and species hybrids.

Usually a few other characteristics are ascribed to cross-breeds by which they are distinguished from the hybrids of species. Gärtner has asserted that cross-breeds of like descent are even in the first generation very dissimilar, while hybrids of the first generation are always very uniform. This assertion, which is also repeated by others, is entirely wrong. The polymorphism of the hybrids of the species of Abutilon, Passiflora, Hieracium, etc., has already been shown, while, on the other hand, the crosses of races, in the first generation, are usually just as uniform as the real hybrids. Again, it has sometimes been asserted that the "varieties" of one and the same species, when crossed with another species, always produce the same hybrid forms. Gärtner, especially, has laid particular stress upon this supposed behavior of varieties, although he must have known that Kölreuter had already observed the inheritance of color of the blossom in the races of Mirabilis, Dianthus, and Verbascum, the doubling of flowers in Aquilegia and Dianthus, the carriage and form of the leaf in the races of Nicotiana Tabacum and Hibiscus. The white-blossoming Datura ferox gives with D. Stramonium a white-blooming cross, and with the smooth-fruited race (var. Bertolonii) of the same species, a blue-blossoming cross. Nymphaea Lotus × rubra is different from N. Lotus × dentata. It cannot be in the least doubtful that the inheritable characteristics of races and so-called varieties are also bequeathed to their progeny.

One will hardly go wrong if he assumes that Gärtner came to make this rule about the behavior of varieties through the behavior of unfixed garden crosses and garden sorts. It is a matter of course that forms which show themselves unfixed in their normal progeny should produce polymorphous hybrids, and that unfixed variety-signs are apt to disappear entirely in the products of crossing with pure species.

The true situation is, in short, as follows: — The nearer the morphological and systematic relationship of the parent forms is, the less the sexual capacity of reproduction in the cross is apt to depart from the normal direction; the greater the difference between the parent forms, the more, on the average, is the fruitfulness of the cross weakened. Exceptions are not rare.

The nearer the parent forms are related to each other, the oftener the progeny of crosses show complete returns to the parent forms.

Crosses from nearly related parent forms sometimes show in their blossoms and fruits the peculiar characteristics of the parent forms unmixed beside each other; this rarely takes place in crosses whose parent forms were considerably different. Most unsymmetrically colored flowers (Mirabilis, Camellia, Mimulus, Petunia, etc.) first originated in the progeny of crosses.

LECTURE V.

POLLINATION; OR HOW TO CROSS PLANTS.

1. THE STRUCTURE OF THE FLOWER.

POLLINATION is the act of conveying pollen from the anther to the stigma. It is the manual part of the crossing of plants. The word fertilization is often used in a like sense, although erroneously; for it is the office of the pollen, not of the operator, to fertilize or fecundate that part of the flower which is to develop into a seed.

The chief requirement in pollinating flowers is to know the parts of the flower itself. The con-

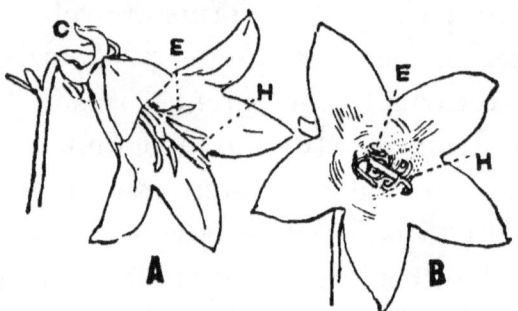

FIG. 1. — Bell-flower.

spicuous or showy part of the flower is the *envelope*, which is endlessly modified in size, form, and color.

This envelope protects the inner or essential organs, and it also attracts insects, which often perform the labor of pollination. This floral envelope is usually of two series or parts,—an outer and commonly green series known as the *calyx*, and an inner and generally more showy series known as the *corolla*. These two series are well shown in the bell-flower, Fig. 1. The calyx, with its reflexed lobes, is at C, and the large bell-form portion is the corolla. When the calyx is composed of separate parts or leaves, each part is called a *sepal*; in like manner each separate part of the corolla is a *petal*. In the lily, Fig. 2, there is no distinction between calyx and corolla; or, it may be said, the calyx is wanting. These envelopes of the flower are often much disguised. This is particularly true in the orchids, one of which, a lady-slipper, is illustrated in Fig. 3. The sepals are seen at DD. They are apparently only two, but there is reason to believe that the lower sepal

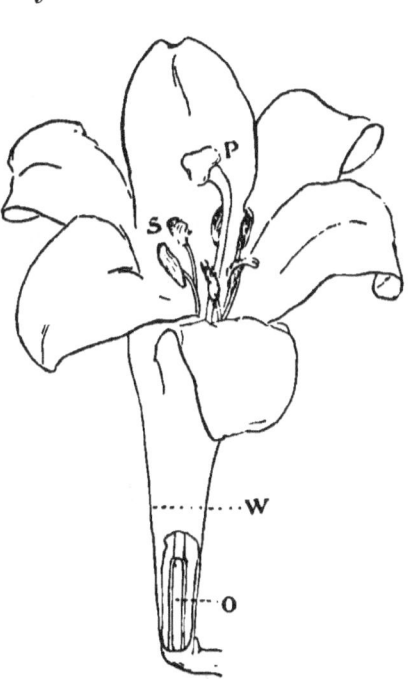

FIG. 2.— Flower of white lily.

is really made up of a union of two. The three inner leaves are the petals, the lower one, H, being enlarged into the sac or slipper.

The most important organs of the flower, however, to one who wishes to make crosses, are the so-called sexual organs, the stamens and pistils. They can be readily distinguished in the lily, Fig. 2. The six bodies shown at S are the ends of the *stamens*, or so-called male organs. These stamens generally have a stalk or stem, known as a *filament*, and the enlarged tip as the *anther*. It is in this anther that the pollen is borne. The pollen is generally made up of very minute yellow or brownish grains, although it is sometimes in the form of a more or less glutinous or adhesive mass, as in the milk-weeds and orchids. The irritating dust which falls from the corn tassels at the later cultivatings is the pollen.

FIG. 3.—Flower of greenhouse cypripedium.

The *pistil*, or so-called female organ, is shown at OP, Fig. 2. The enlarged portion at O is the *ovary*, which will develop into the seed-pod. The *stigma*, or the enlarged and roughened part which receives the pollen, is at P. Between these two parts is the slender *style*, a portion which is absent in many flowers.

The stamens and pistils are known as the *essential organs* of the flower, for, whilst the calyx and corolla may be entirely absent, either one or both of these organs is present; and these are the parts which are directly concerned in the reproduction of the species. Like the floral envelopes, these essential organs are often greatly modified, so much so that botanists are sometimes perplexed to distinguish them from each other or from modified forms of the petals or sepals. The particular features of these organs which the plant-breeder must be able to distinguish are the anther and the stigma; for the anther bears the pollen, and the stigma must receive it. In Fig. 1, the stamens are shown at E. In the flower A, which has just expanded, these stamens are rigid and in condition to shed the pollen, but in the flower B, they have shed the pollen and have collapsed. The stigma in this case is divided into three parts, but when the flower first opens, these parts are closed together, H in flower A, so that it is impossible that they receive any pollen from the same flower;

when the stamens have withered, however, as in B, the stigma, H, spreads open and is ready to

FIG. 4.—Flower of night-blooming cereus.

receive any pollen which may be brought to it by insects or other agencies. In this case, the ovary or young seed-pod, which is in the bottom of the flower, is not shown in the engraving.

Some of the particular forms of essential organs are well illustrated in the accompanying photographs. In the night-blooming cereus, Fig. 4, the many-rayed stigma is shown just below the

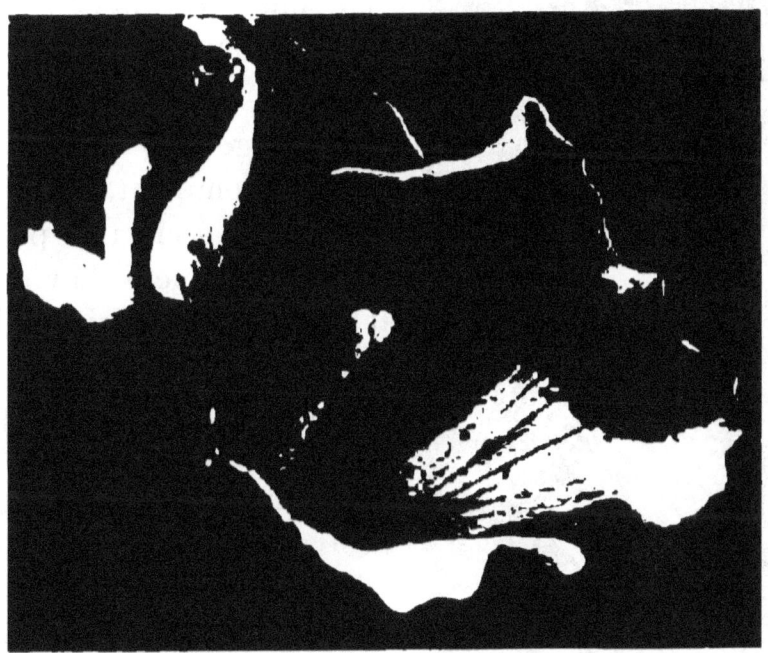

Fig. 5. — Flower of the shrubby hibiscus (Hibiscus Syriacus).

centre of the mouth of the flower, and the numerous stamens are arranged in a circular manner outside of it. The many petals and numerous spreading sepals are also well shown. The hibiscus, Fig. 5, has a central column with the anthers hanging upon it, and a large stigma raised beyond

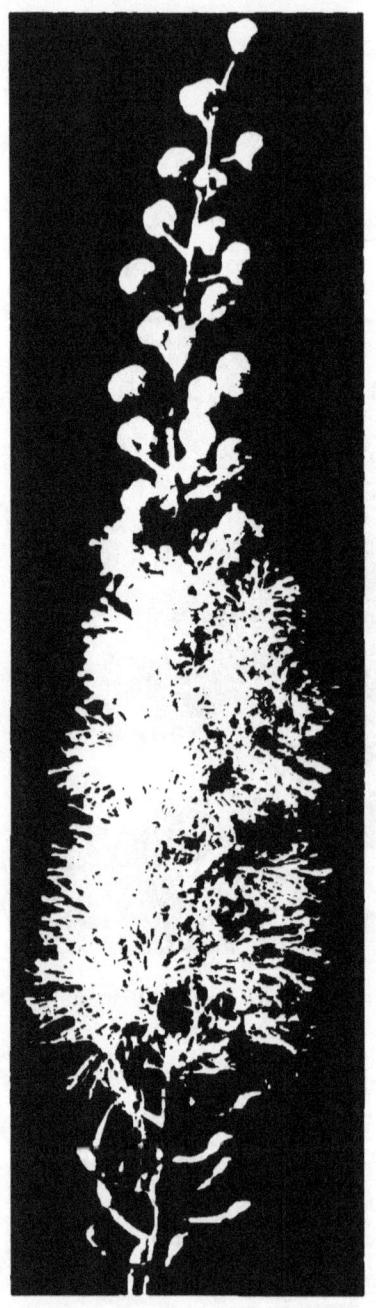

Fig. 6. — Bugbane (Cimicifuga racemosa).

them. The wild bugbane, or cimicifuga, is seen in Fig. 6, natural size. Here is a long spike or cluster of flowers. At the top are the unopened buds, in the centre the expanded flowers with the floral envelopes fallen away, — the fringe-like stamens very prominent, — and below are seen the pistils, the stamens having fallen. These pistils will now ripen into pods, but the tip-like stigma may still be seen on them. The stamens and the long protruding style, tipped with its stigma, are also shown in the fuchsia, Fig. 15. The essential organs of orchids are curiously disguised. They are combined into a single body. In the lady-slipper, Fig. 3, the lip-like stigma is shown at P. Upon either side, at its base, is an anther S. Projecting over the stigma is a greenish ladle-like body, T, which is a transformed and sterile anther. In all lady-slippers, these organs are essentially the same as in the drawing, although they vary much in size and shape; but in most other orchids, the two side anthers, S, are wholly wanting, and the terminal organ, T, is a pollen-bearing anther. In numerous plants, there are many distinct pistils in each flower. Such is the case in the strawberry, where each little yellow "seed" on the ripened berry represents a pistil; and the blackberry and the raspberry, where each little grain or drupelet of the fruit stands for the same organ. A flowering raspberry is illustrated natural size in Fig. 7, for the purpose of showing the ring of many anthers near the centre of the flower, inside of which, in the very centre, is a little head of pistils.

It frequently occurs that the stamens and pistils are borne in different flowers, rather than together in the same flower as they are in the examples which we have studied. In these cases the flower is said to be staminate, or male or sterile, in one case, and pistillate, female or fertile, in the other case. If these two kinds of flowers are borne together upon the same plant, as in pumpkins, melons, cucumbers, chestnuts, oaks, and begonias, the plant is said to be *monœcious;* but if the staminate and pistillate flowers are on entirely different plants, as in willows and poplars, the plant is *diœcious*. The two kinds of squash flowers are shown in Fig. 8. The pistillate flower is on the left, and it is at once distinguished by the ovary or little squash below the colored portion,

Fig. 7. — Blossom of flowering raspberry (Rubus odoratus).

or corolla of the flower. The lobed stigma is seen in the centre. The staminate flower is on the right. It has a longer stem, no ovary, and the anthers are united into a conspicuous cone in the centre. The flowers expand early in the morning. Insects carry pollen to the pistillate flower, which

STAMINATE AND PISTILLATE FLOWERS. 261

then begins to set its fruit, whilst the staminate flower dies. The flowers of the common wild clematis are shown in Fig. 9. Upon the right

Fig. 8. — Squash flowers of each sex.

are the sterile flowers, which are wholly staminate. On the left, the flowers with larger sepals — the petals are absent — have a cone of pistils in the centre, and a few short and sterile stamens spreading from the base of the cone. These different flowers are borne on different plants in this species of clematis, and the plants are therefore practically diœcious, because the stamens of the pistillate flowers generally bear no pollen. A similar mixed arrangement occurs in some strawber-

Fig. 9. — Flowers of clematis (Clematis Virginiana).

ries, except that there are no purely staminate flowers. There are purely pistillate varieties, others, like the Crescent, with a few nearly or quite abortive stamens at the base of the cone of pistils, and others in which the flowers are perfect or hermaphrodite, that is, containing the two sexes.

The compositous flowers — like the asters, daisies, goldenrods, sunflowers, dahlias, zinnias, chrysanthemums, and their kin — need to be considered in still a different category. In these plants, the head, or so-called flower, is an aggregation of several or many small flowers or florets. Each seed in a sunflower head, for example, represents a distinct flower. Sometimes all of these flowers are perfect, — contain the two sexes, — and sometimes they are pistillate or staminate in different parts of the head; and in some cases the plants are diœcious. In many plants of the composite family, the flowers near the border of the head are unlike those of the centre or disc, in having a long ray-like corolla; and these ray-flowers are frequently of different form from the others in the character of the essential organs. Very frequently the ray-flowers are pistillate, whilst the disc-flowers are generally hermaphrodite. The anthers, in these plants, are united in a ring closely about the style and below the stigma.

The ovary, as we have seen, ripens into the pod, berry, or other fruit; but it is not able to bear seeds until it is assisted by the pollen. The pollen falls upon the roughish or sticky surface of the stigma, and there germinates or sends a minute tube downwards through the style and finally reaches the ovule, which, when fertilized, rapidly ripens into the seed. The nature of this fecundation is not germane to the present subject; but it may be said that only one pollen grain is necessary to the fertilization of a single ovule, but the addition of a superabundance of pollen greatly stimulates the growth of the fleshy or enveloping parts of the fruit. It is important that the person who desires to cross plants should become familar with the stigma when it is "ripe," receptive, or ready to receive the pollen. This condition is generally indicated by the glutinous or sticky or moist condition of the stigma, or in those stigmas which are not glutinous it is told by the appearing of a distinctly roughened or papillose condition. This receptive condition generally occurs about as soon as the flower opens. If pollen is withheld, the stigma will remain receptive much longer than when fertilization has taken place, — in some flowers for two or three days.

The pollen is discharged from the anther in various ways, but it most commonly escapes through a chink or crack in the side of the anther. Sometimes it escapes through pores at one end of the anther; and in other cases there are more elaborate mechanisms to admit of its discharge. In most plants, the anthers and stigma in the same flower mature at different times, so that close-fertilization or in-breeding is avoided. This is well illustrated in the bell-flower, Fig. 1. Here the anthers wither and die before the stigmatic lobes open. In other cases, the stigma matures first, although this is not the usual condition.

II. Manipulating the Flowers.

We are now familiar with the essential principles in the pollination of flowers. Before a person proceeds to operate upon a flower with which he is unfamiliar, he should carefully study its structure, so as to be able to locate the different organs, and to discover when the pollen and the stigma are ready for the work.

The first and last rule in the pollinating of plants is this: *Exercise every precaution to prevent any other pollination than that which you design to give.* The anthers, therefore, must be removed from the flower *before it opens.* This removal of the anthers is known as *emasculation.* Just as soon as this is done, tie up the flower securely in a bag to protect it from foreign pollen which may be brought by wind or insects. As soon as the stigma is ripe, remove the bag and apply the desired pollen, placing the bag on the flower again, where it must remain until the seeds begin to form. The stigma may be receptive the day following emasculation, or, perhaps, not until a week afterwards. Much depends upon the age of the bud when emasculation takes place. It is generally best to delay emasculation as long as possible and not have the flower open; but the operator must be sure that the anthers do not discharge or that insects do not get into the flower before he has emasculated it. The bud at B, in Fig. 3, is

Fig. 10.— Tobacco flowers, showing the parts of the flower, a bud ready to be emasculated, and an emasculated subject.

nearly ready to emasculate. The older buds on the top of the spike of bugbane, Fig. 6, are ready to operate upon; and so is the bud seen at the left in Fig. 7.

The manner of emasculating the flower varies

with the operator. It is a common practice to clip off the anthers with a pair of small scissors, or to hook them out with a bent pin or a crochet hook. Others use tweezers. For myself, however, I do not like any of these methods, because the anthers are apt to drop into the bottom of the corolla, where it is sometimes difficult to rescue them; and if one uses tweezers, there is always danger that the anthers may be crushed and that some of the pollen may adhere to the instrument and contaminate future crosses. I therefore usually cut the corolla completely off just above the ovary, with a pair of small, long-handled surgeon's scissors (see Fig. 12), removing everything but the pistil. The operation is explained in Fig. 10, which shows the tobacco flower. The flower at the left shows the pin-head stigma in the centre of the throat, and the five anthers surrounding it. The second flower is spread open for the purpose of showing these organs. The third figure is a bud in the right condition for operation. The right-hand figure shows this bud cut around with the points of the scissors, leaving only the pistil. The line at W, in Fig. 2, shows where the flower of the lily might be cut off. The manner of operating upon a compositous flower is shown in the picture of the zinnia, Fig. 11. In this plant the outer florets of the head are pistillate, whilst those of the disc are perfect. It is only necessary,

268   POLLINATION.

therefore, to remove the central stamen-bearing flowers before any of them open, and to cover the flower up before any of the pistils near the border

Fig. 11. -- Zinnia flowers; the upper head ready for emasculation, the lower one showing the operation performed.

have protruded themselves. The upper head in Fig. 11 shows the untreated sample, whilst the lower one shows the same with the cone of central flowers pulled out. This treated head should now be covered, to await the maturing of the stigmas. In many compositous plants, however, the case is not so simple as this, because all the flowers are perfect. In such cases, nearly all the florets should be removed from the head, and a few remaining ones emasculated in essentially the same manner as described for the tobacco, Fig. 10. Whenever flowers are borne in clusters, nearly all of them should be removed and the attention confined to only two or three of them. One is then more certain of getting seeds to set. In some cases, like the apple cluster, only one or two flowers of any cluster ever set fruit, and the operator should then choose the two or three strongest and most promising buds, and cut all the others off.

Flowers which bear no stamens, as the pistillate flowers of squashes, strawberries, and many other plants, of course do not require emasculating. They should be tied up while in bud, however, to prevent the access of any foreign pollen. Indian corn is a case in point. The pistillate flowers are on the ear, each kernel of corn representing a single flower. The silks are the stigmas. If it is desired to cross corn, therefore, the ear should be covered before any silks are protruded, and the pollen should be applied some days later, when the silks are full grown. The staminate or male flowers are in the tassel.

270   POLLINATION.

The pollen should be derived from a flower which has also been protected from wind and in-

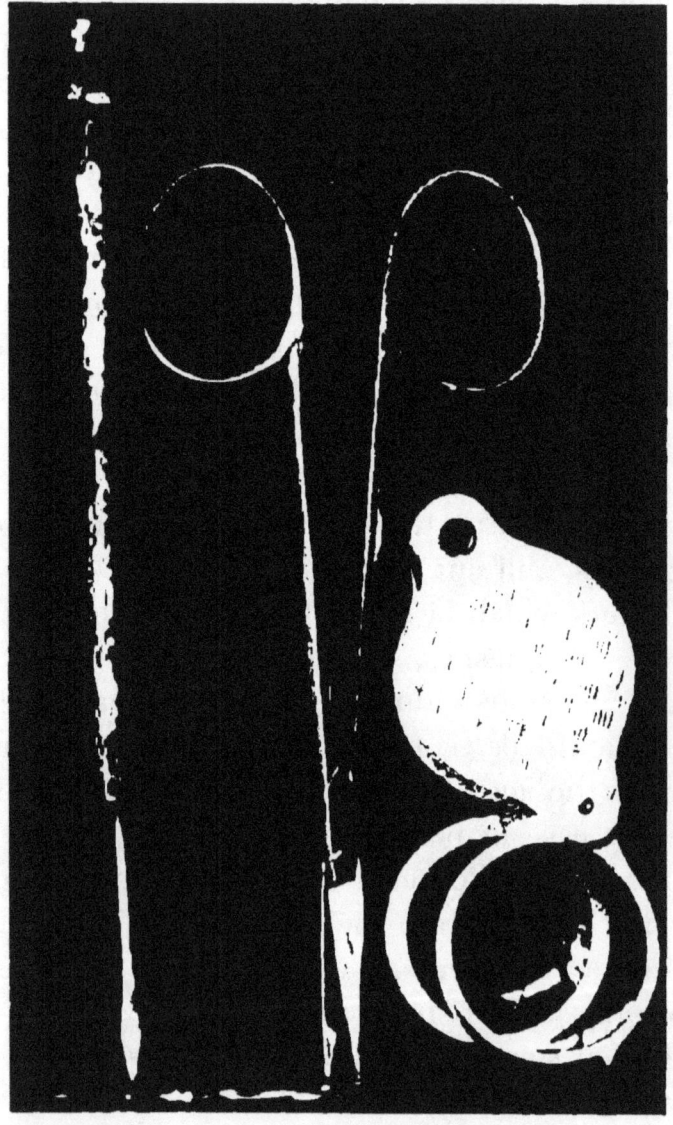

FIG. 12. — Instruments used in pollinating flowers, natural size. Pin scalpel, scissors, lens.

sects, because foreign pollen may have been dropped upon an anther by an insect visitor and it may be unknowingly transferred by the operator. The pollen-bearing parent needs no operation, of course, but the flower should have been tied up in a bag when it was in bud. The pollen is best obtained by picking off a ripe anther and crushing it upon the thumb-nail. Then it is transferred to the stigma by a tiny scalpel made by hammering out the small end of a pin, as shown, full size, at the left in Fig. 12. The stigma should be *entirely covered* with the pollen, if possible. It is often advised to use a camel's hair

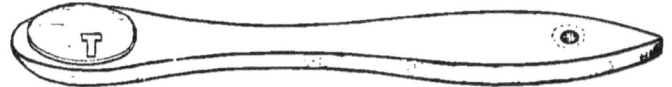

Fig. 13.—Ladle for pollinating house tomatoes.

brush to transfer the pollen, but much of the pollen sticks amongst the hairs of the brush and is ready to contaminate a future cross; and where the pollen is scarce it cannot be conserved to advantage by a brush. In some cases the pollen is discharged so freely that the anther may be rubbed upon the stigma, or even shaken over it, but in most instances it will be necessary to actually place the pollen upon the stigma with some hard instrument. When pollinating house-grown melons and cucumbers, the staminate flower is broken off, the corolla stripped back, and the anther-cone inserted into the pistillate flower, where it is allowed to remain until it dries and falls away. In pollinating house tomatoes, an implement shown in Fig. 13, one-third size, is used. This is simply a watch-glass, T, secured to a handle. When the house is dry, at midday, the watch-glass is held under the flowers, which are tapped, and the pollen falls into the glass. The glass is then held up under another flower until the stigma rests in the pollen. It should be said, however, that this pollination of tomatoes is for the purpose of making the fruit set in the absence of insects, not to effect a cross. If the latter purpose were the object sought, the flowers which are to bear the seeds would need to be emasculated.

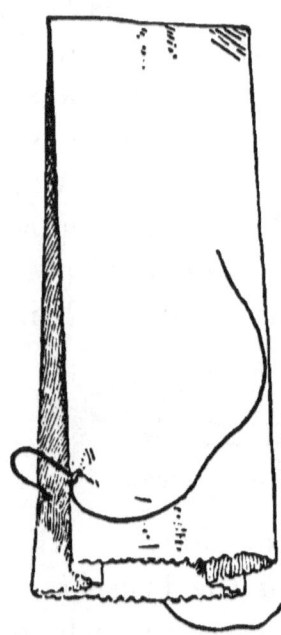

FIG. 14.—Bag for covering the flowers.

Sometimes it is impossible to secure the pollen at the time the stigma is ready. In some cases of this kind, the intended parents can be grown under glass so as to bring them into bloom at the same time. In other cases, it is necessary to keep the pollen for some time. The length of time that pollen will keep varies with the species and probably also with the strength and vigor of the plant which bears it. As a rule, it will not keep more than a week or two, and, in general, it may

Fig. 15. — Fuchsias, showing the stamens and pistils, and a bud ready to be emasculated.

be said that the fresher it is the better it may be expected to act. It is best kept in dry and tight

T

paper bags, such as are used for covering the flowers.

Something more should be said about the bags which are used for covering the flowers. After having tried every kind which is recommended, I find grocer's manilla bags much the most satisfactory. For most flowers the four-ounce size is the handiest. When the bags are still flat, as

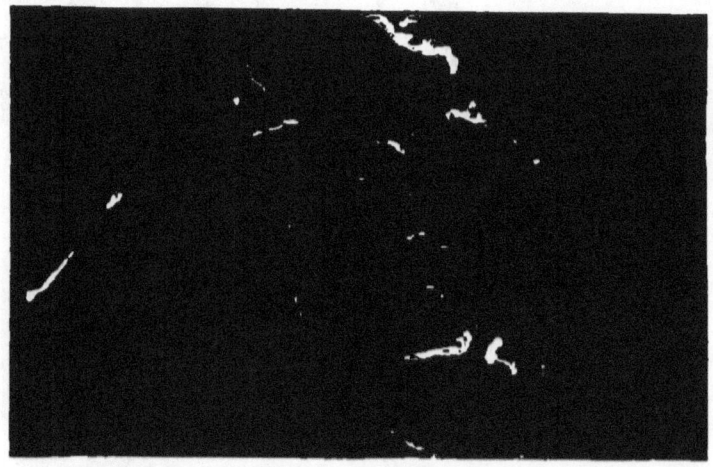

Fig. 16.— Fuchsia flower emasculated.

they come from the packages, a hole is made through the two overlapping folds near the opening, and a string is passed through it and then tied at one of the folds, as shown in Fig. 14. The bag is then ready for use. Before it is put on the flower, the lower end of it is dipped in water to soften it so that it can be puckered tightly about the stem and thereby prevent the entrance of any insect. A bag is put upon the seed-bearing flower when emasculation is performed, and upon the intended pollen parent when the flower is still in bud. The bag may be removed from the emasculated flower from time to time to examine the stigma, and again when the pollen is applied; but it should not be taken off permanently until the pod or fruit begins to grow.

By way of recapitulation, let us consider the crossing of a fuchsia flower. In Fig. 15 two flowers are shown in full bloom, with the long style and the eight shorter stamens. The single

Fig. 17.— Fuchsia flower tied up after emasculation.

bud is just the right age to emasculate. We therefore cut off the two flowers and emasculate the bud, as in Fig. 16. The pollen of another flower is applied and the bag is tied on, as seen in Fig. 17. The best label is a small merchandise tag, and this records the staminate parent and the date.

It will be seen that in the operation of emasculating the fuchsia flower we cut off the sepals as

FIG. 18. — Tomato and quince, showing how the sepals were cut off in emasculating.

well as the petals. In some plants the calyx adheres to the full-grown fruit, as on the apple, pear, quince, gooseberry, or persists at the base of the fruit, as in the tomato, pea, raspberry. In these fruits, therefore, the cutting away of the calyx leaves an indelible mark which at once distinguishes the fruits which have been crossed, even if the labels are lost. In Fig. 18 a tomato and quince are shown which are thus marked.

All the foregoing remarks do not apply to the crossing of ferns, lycopods, and the like, because these plants have no flowers; yet cross-fertilization may take place in them. When the spores

Fig. 19. — Pollinating kit.

of these flowerless plants are sown, a thin green tissue, or prothallus, appears and spreads over the ground. In this tissue the separate sex-organs appear, and after fecundation takes place, the fern, as we commonly understand it, springs forth. Thereafter, this fern lives an asexual life and produces spores year after year; but it is only in this primitive prothallic stage that fertilization takes place, once in the lifetime of the plant. If these plants are to be crossed, the only procedure open to the gardener is to sow the spores of the intended parents together in the hope that a natural mixing may take place. There are various well-authenticated fern hybrids.

The pollination of flowers is such a simple work that few implements are required for its easy performance. Great care is more important than

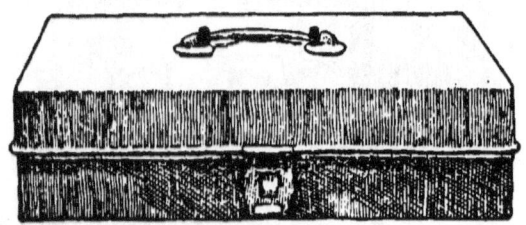

Fig. 20. — Pollinating kit.

any number of tools. Every one who expects to cross plants should provide himself with the three instruments shown in Fig. 12, — a pin scalpel, sharp-pointed scissors, and a large hand-lens. If one contemplates much experimenting in this direction, however, it is economy of time to have some sort of a box in which there are compartments for the various necessities. These various compartments suggest at once whatever accessories are wanting, and they hold a sufficient supply for several hundred operations. There should be a compartment for bags, string, lens, scissors, and pencils, tags, note-book, and the like. Figs. 19 and 20 show a convenient case for an experimenter, and one which I have used with satisfaction for several years. This kit is twelve inches long, nine inches wide, and three inches deep.

The chances of success in pollinating are discussed in Lecture II. (page 83).

GLOSSARY.

1. THE FLOWER.

Anther. — That portion of the stamen which bears the pollen. It is the uppermost portion of the stamen.

Calyx. — The outer series of floral envelopes, usually green. The various separate parts of the calyx are sepals.

Corolla. — The inner series of floral envelopes, usually colored and forming the showy part of the flower. If it is divided into separate parts, these are called petals.

Essential organs. — The stamens and pistils.

Female. — Said of flowers which have only pistils or the seed-bearing part, or of plants which bear only such flowers; applied also to the pistils in any flower.

Filament. — The stalk or stem of a stamen, bearing the anther.

Floral envelopes. — The calyx and corolla.

Male. — Said of flowers which bear only stamens, or of plants which have only staminate flowers; also applied to the stamens or pollen-bearing organs of flowers.

Ovary. — The lowest part of the pistil, containing the ovules. It is the most thickened portion of the pistil, and it may stand either below or above the petals. The ovary ripens into the fruit.

Ovule. — A body in the ovary which ripens into a seed.

Pet'-al. — The separate portions or leaves of the corolla.

Pistil. — The seed-bearing organ of the flower. It always comprises two parts, the ovary — which becomes the pod or fruit — and the stigma. Usually there is a style connecting the two. Often called the fertile or female organ.

Pistillate. — Said of a plant or flower which has only pistils or female organs.

Pollen. — The contents of the anther, capable of fertilizing the ovules. It is usually composed of minute yellow or brown grains.

Se'-pal. — The separate portions or leaves of the calyx.

Spore. — The reproductive organ of flowerless plants, by means of which they propagate, as other plants propagate by means of the seed. The spore is asexual.

Stamen. — The pollen-bearing organ of the flower. Often called the male or sterile organ. Its essential part is the anther. The stalk, when present, is called the filament.

Staminate. — Said of a flower or plant which bears only stamens or male organs.

Stigma. — The top end of the pistil, where the pollen lodges and germinates. It is usually a somewhat expanded surface, and is roughened, or sticky, or moist when ready to receive the pollen.

Style. — The more or less slender portion of the pistil which lies between the stigma and ovary. The pollen-tubes pass through it in reaching the ovary.

2. CROSSING.

Bigener; bigeneric-hybrid. — A hybrid between species of different genera.

Bigeneric half-breed. — The product of a cross between varieties of species of different genera.

Close-fertilization; self-fertilization. — The action of pollen upon the pistil of the same flower.

Close-pollination: self-pollination. — The transfer of pollen to a pistil of the same flower.

Cross. — The offspring of any two flowers which have been cross-fertilized.

GLOSSARY. 283

Cross-breed; half-breed; mongrel; variety-hybrid. — A cross between varieties of the same species.

Cross-fertilization. — The action of pollen upon the pistil of another flower of the same species.

Crossing. — The operation or practice of cross-pollinating.

Cross-pollination. — The conveyance of pollen to the stigma of another flower.

Derivative- or derivation-hybrid; secondary-hybrid. — A hybrid between hybrids, or between a hybrid and one of its parents.

Fertilization; fecundation; impregnation. — The action of the pollen upon the ovules.

Half-hybrid. — The product of a cross between a species and a variety of another species.

Hybrid. — The offspring of crossed plants of different species.

Hybridism; hybridity. — The state, quality, or condition of being a hybrid.

Hybridization. — The state or condition of being hybridized, or the process or act of hybridizing.

Hybridizing. — The operation or practice of crossing between species.

Individual cross. — The offspring of two crossed flowers on the same plant.

Individual fertilization. — Fertilization between flowers upon the same plant.

Mongrel. — A cross.

Mule. — A sterile (seedless) hybrid.

Pollination. — The conveyance of pollen from the anther to the stigma (page 252).

The term *cross* is used to denote the offspring of any sexual union between plants, whether of different species or varieties, or even different flowers upon the same plant. It is a general term. And the word is also sometimes used to denote the operation of performing or bringing about the sexual union. There are different kinds of crosses. One of these is the *hybrid*. A hybrid is a cross between two species, as a plum and a peach, or a raspberry and a blackberry. There has lately been some objection urged against this term, because it is often impossible to define the limitations of species,—to tell where one species ends and another begins. And it is a fact that this difficulty exists, for plants which some botanists regard as mere varieties others regard as distinct species. But the term *hybrid* is no more inaccurate than the term *species*, upon which it rests; and, so long as men talk about species, so long have we an equal right to talk about hybrids. Here, as everywhere, terms are mere conveniences, and they seldom express the whole truth. In common speech the word *hybrid* is much misused. Crosses between varieties of one species are termed *half-breeds* or *cross-breeds*, and those between different flowers upon the same plant are called *individual crosses*.

3. CLASSIFICATION.

Break. — A radical departure from the type. Ordinarily used in the sense of *sport*, but in its larger meaning it refers to the permanent appearance of apparently new or very pronounced characters in a species.

Bud-variation. — Variation or departure from a type through the agency of buds (pages 28, 153).

Bud-variety. — A variety resulting from bud-variation. Bud-sport.

Family (*Order* in botany.) — A group of genera and species; as *Cupuliferæ*, the Oak Family, *Rosaceæ*, the Rose Family.

Form. — A minor variety, usually transient, produced by some local environment.

Genus (plural, *genera*). — A group or kind comprising a greater or less number of closely related species; as *Acer*, the maples, *Fragaria*, the strawberries.

Race. — A fixed cultural variety; that is, a cultural variety which reproduces itself more or less uniformly from seeds.

Seedling. — A plant growing directly from seed, without the intervention of grafts, layers, or cuttings.

Seed-variation. — Variation or departure from a type through the agency of seeds.

Seed-variety. — A variety resulting from seed-variation.

Species (plural, *species*). — An indefinite term applied to all individuals of a certain kind which come or are supposed to come from a common parentage. A perennial succession of normal or natural similar individuals perpetuated by means of seedage. "All the descendants from the same stock." — *Gray*.

Sport. — A variety or variation which appears suddenly and unaccountably, either from seeds or buds; more properly restricted to varieties originating from buds, and so used in this book.

Stock. — The parentage of a particular strain or variety.

Strain. — A sub-variety, or individuals of a variety, which has been improved and bred under known conditions.

Variation. — 1. The act or condition of varying or becoming modified. 2. A transient variety, more or less incapable of being fixed or rendered permanent.

Variety. — A form or series of forms of a species marked by characters of less permanence or less importance than are the species themselves.

Wilding. — A wild individual from a cultivated species.

INDEX.

Abortive varieties, 152.
Abutilon, crosses, 220, 233, 250.
Accident, 154.
Acclimatization, 24, 26.
Acer, bud-variety, 177.
Achimenes, crosses, 245, 246, 247.
Acorns, bud-variety, 177.
Acquired characters, 14.
Adult forms, 156.
Ægilops, crosses, 243.
Æsculus, bud-variety, 178.
Æsculus, crosses, 239.
Agathæa, bud-variety, 178.
Ageratum, bud-varieties, 178.
Agrostemma Cœli-rosa, dwarfs, 144.
Albinos, 148.
Allut, Cazalis, 211.
Almond, bud-variety, 179.
Alnus, crosses, 226.
Alopecurus, crosses, 230.
Altitude and plants, 25.
Amelioration, gradual, 50.
Amygdalus, crosses, 239.
Anagallis, crosses, 222, 223, 231.
Anemone, crosses, 224, 229.
Anemone, varieties, 179.
Animal and plant contrasted, 5, 91.
Année, 141.
Antagonistic features, 95.
Anther, 254.
Apple, Wealthy, 108.
Apples, bud-variation in, 118, 175.
Apples, hybrid, 66, 79, 111.
Apples, races of, 90.
Apples, variations in, 3, 27, 37, 99, 131.
Apricot, bud-variety, 179.
Aquilegia, crosses, 224, 229, 234, 239, 240, 250.

Aralia, bud-variety, 180.
Arthur, 103, 116.
Arundo, variation, 176, 180.
Asexual propagation, 7.
Aspidistra, sport, 180.
Aster, varieties, 180.
Atavism, 106.
Atragene, 184.
Atropa, crosses, 223.
Azalea, bud-varieties, 180.

Bag for covering flowers, 272.
Bamboos, variation, 176.
Banana, varieties, 175.
Bartel, T. C., 130.
Barteldes, 140.
Bean, bud-variation, 176.
Beans, types of, 135.
Beet, crosses, 56.
Begonia, crosses, 224, 226, 227, 229, 230, 231, 233, 234, 239, 245, 246, 247.
Begonia pollinations, 86.
Bell-flower, 252.
Berberis, crosses, 245.
Bigness, variation in, 18.
Blackberry, crosses, 79, 111.
Blackberry, introduction of, 129.
Bletia, crosses, 222.
Bohnhof, 80.
Bornet, 232.
Bouschet, Henri, 212.
Brassica, crosses, 223, 239, 240, 241.
Braun, Alexander, 17.
Breaking the type, 19, 23, 93.
Bruant, 113.
Buckwheat, crosses, 56.
Budd, Professor, 133.

288 INDEX.

Bud-variation, 6, 21, 28, 37, 101, 118, 126, 153.
Bugbane, 258.
Burpee, 139.
Buxus, bud-varieties, 181.

Cabbage, crosses, 56.
Cacti, crosses, 235.
Calceolaria, crosses, 222, 229, 233, 234, 239, 245, 247.
Calceolaria plantaginea, dwarfs, 144.
Calliopsis tinctoria, dwarfs, 144.
Callistephus hortensis, dwarfs, 145.
Calyx, 253.
Camellia, bud-varieties, 182.
Camellia, crosses, 251.
Canary-grass, crosses, 57.
Cannas, 140.
Capsella, crosses, 226, 231.
Carman, 79.
Carnation, 115.
Carrière, 96, 116, 153.
Caspary, 229.
Cedars, 156.
Cephalotaxus, sports, 183.
Cereus, bud-variety, 184.
Cereus, crosses, 226, 230, 233, 239.
Cereus, night-blooming, 256.
Change of seed, 28, 59, 116.
Checking growth, 116.
Cheiranthus, sport of, 185.
Cherry, hybrid, 112.
Cherry, sports of, 171.
Chloranthic varieties, 153.
Chlorosis, 149.
Choice of variations, 31.
Chrysanthemum carinatum, 100.
Chrysanthemum, sports of, 158.
Cimicifuga racemosa, 258.
Cinchona, crosses, 225.
Cirsium, crosses, 229, 233, 239.
Cistus, crosses, 219, 222, 231, 234.
Clematis, crosses, 224.
Clematis, flowers, 262.
Clematis, varieties, 184.
Climate and variation, 24, 114, 146.
Coleus, sports in, 120.
Coloration, 148.
Colors, modified by climate, 25.
Coniferæ, 156.

Contradictory attributes, 98.
Convolvulus pollinations, 85.
Coreopsis tinctoria, dwarfs, 144.
Cornus, bud-varieties, 185.
Corolla, 253.
Cotyledon, crosses, 229.
Crabs, hybrid, 66, 111.
Cratægus, crosses, 239.
Crinum, crosses, 218, 225, 229, 232, 234.
Cross-breeds, Focke on, 247.
Cross, function of, 50.
Cross, primary, 215.
Crosses, characteristics of, 68.
Crosses, Focke on, 215.
Crossing a means, 107.
Crossing and change of seed, 59.
Crossing, limits of, 44.
Crossing, philosophy of, 39.
Crossing, rule for, 109.
Crozy, 113, 140.
Cucumber pollinations, 85.
Cucumis, crosses, 222.
Cucurbita Pepo, 75, 84.
Cucurbitaceæ, crosses, 46, 58, 74, 82, 229, 230, 235.
Cultivation, philosophy of, 22.
Currant, sports of, 173. (See Ribes.)
Cypripedium, 254.
Cypripedium, crosses, 218, 227, 229, 246.
Cytisus Adami, 185.

Dactylis, bud-variety, 185.
Darwin, 17, 23, 32, 42, 47, 51, 54, 56, 60, 63, 69, 72, 84, 87, 117, 119, 121, 176, 228.
Dating back, 106.
Datura, crosses, 222, 223, 224, 226, 228, 234, 239, 240, 249, 250.
Decaisne, 229.
De Candolle, 150, 178.
Derivative crosses, 238.
Dewberry crosses, 79, 111.
Dewberry, introduction of, 129.
Dianthus Chinensis, dwarfs, 145.
Dianthus, crosses, 218, 219, 223, 226, 227, 229, 233, 234, 237, 239, 240, 243, 244, 245, 246, 250.
Dianthus semperflorens, 156.
Dichroism, 154.

INDEX. 289

Digitalis, crosses, 218, 219, 221, 223, 226, 227, 229, 230, 232, 237.
Dimorphism, 154.
Diœcious plants, 260.
Divergence of character, 23.
Division of labor, 42.
Doubleness in hybrids, 237.
Doubleness of flowers, 149.
Dracæna, variation, 176.
Duval, M., 167.
Dwarfing, 25, 114, 143.

Early varieties, 146.
Echinocactus, sports, 186.
Eckford, 113.
Egg-plant, crosses, 57, 74.
Egg-plant pollinations, 85.
Egg-plants, variation in, 95.
Egypt, plagues of, 40.
Elæagnus, bud-varieties, 186.
Emasculation, 265.
Envelopes, floral, 252.
Environment and variation, 12.
Epilobium, crosses, 218, 222, 229, 230, 233.
Equilibrium of organisms, 20, 61.
Erica, crosses, 229, 233, 239, 240, 246, 247.
Essential organs, 255.
Euonymus Japonicus, 156, 186.

Fagus, fern-leaved, 187.
Fall sowing, 115, 143.
Ferns, crossing, 277.
Fertility of soil, 18, 22.
Ficus, forms of, 188.
Filament, 254.
Fittest, survival of, 32, 39.
Fixation of plants, 31.
Flavor, modified by climate, 25.
Flon, M., 156.
Flowerless plants, crossing, 277.
Focke, 68, 81, 108, 215.
Fontanesia, sport, 188.
Food supply, 16, 116.
Fortuitous variation, 9.
Fragaria, crosses, 229.
Fraxinus, bud-varieties, 188.
Fromont, 158.
Fuchsia, crosses, 229, 233, 239, 247.

Fuchsia flowers, 273, 274, 275.
Function of the Cross, 50.
Fusain, 156.

Galium, crosses, 222.
Gardenia, bud-variety, 189.
Gärtner, 216, 218, 219, 220, 228, 233, 235, 239, 240, 243, 244, 248, 249, 250.
Gazania rigens, 146.
Genera, monotypic, 97.
Gesneraceæ, crosses, 227, 229, 246.
Geum, crosses, 219, 229, 239.
Giant forms, 145.
Gibb, Charles, 133.
Gideon, Peter M., 108.
Gillyflower, bud-variety, 189.
Giraud, Désiré, 166.
Gladiolus, crosses, 226, 229, 234, 245, 246.
Gleditschia triacanthos, 207.
Glossary, 282.
Goff, 103.
Gordon, 229, 241, 244.
Gourd, crosses, 58, 74, 82.
Grape, bud-varieties, 174, 210.
Grapes, hybrid, 66, 78, 110, 111.
Gray, Asa, 33, 178.
Greenhouses, produce variation, 115.

Hallock, V. H., & Son, 124.
Hardy varieties, 145.
Hartogia Capensis, 192.
Hedera, forms of, 189.
Helianthemum, crosses, 223, 226.
Helichrysum bracteatum, dwarfs, 144.
Henderson, 138.
Herbert, 248.
Hibiscus, bud-varieties, 190.
Hibiscus, crosses, 225, 250,
Hibiscus Syriacus, 257.
Hieracium, crosses, 220, 233, 234, 237, 239, 250.
Hippeastrum, crosses, 226, 229, 234, 239, 245, 246, 247.
Holly, sports, 191.
Horse-chestnut, bud-variety, 178.
Husk-tomato, 60, 85.
Hyacinth, forms, 190.
Hybrids, characters of, 68, 215.
Hybrids, Focke on, 215.

Hybrids, multiple, 246, 247.
Hybrids, rarity of, 53.
Hybrids, seven-eighths, 243.
Hybrids, three-fourths, 243.
Hybrids, triple, 244.
Hydrangea, 146, 191.
Hymenocallis, crosses, 230.

Iberis umbellata, dwarfs, 145.
Ignotum tomato, 123.
Ilex, bud-varieties, 191.
Impatiens Balsamina, dwarfs, 145.
In-breeding, 72.
Indeterminate varieties, 87.
Individuality, causes of, 8.
Individuality, fact of, 2.
Instruments for pollination, 270.
Ipomœas, colors of seeds, 104.
Iris, bud-variety, 192.
Isolation of the plant, 22.
Isoloma, crosses, 226, 227, 231, 233, 246.
Ivy, forms of, 189.

Jamain, M., 163.
Jobert, M., 179.
Joigneaux, M., 204.
Juniperus, bud-varieties, 192.

Klotzsch, 226, 229.
Knight, Thomas Andrew, 17, 54, 227, 229.
Kohl-rabi, 80.
Kölreuter, 54, 73, 216, 217, 219, 228, 229, 243, 244, 250.
Kumerle, W. J., 140.
Kuntze, 225.

Labor, division of, 42, 48.
Lachaume, M., 166.
Lactuca, crosses, 238.
Ladle for pollinating, 271.
Lamium, bud-variety, 192.
Lamium, crosses, 230, 241.
Lantana, crosses, 222.
Large-flowered varieties, 145.
Late varieties, 146.
Latitude and plants, 25.
Laurocerasus, sports, 192.
Lavatera, crosses, 234, 239, 243.

Leafiness, 25.
Lecoq, 227.
Lemoine, 113.
Lens for pollinating, 270.
Leptosiphon densiflorus, dwarfs, 144.
Lettuce, crosses, 56.
Ligustrum, sports, 193.
Lilac, bud-varieties, 193.
Lily, white, 253.
Lima beans, 138.
Limits of crossing, 44.
Linaria, crosses, 222, 227, 238, 239, 241.
Lindley, 68.
Links, missing, 41, 48.
Linnæus, 81, 152.
Linum, crosses, 223.
Lobelia, crosses, 219, 222, 232, 233, 234, 235, 245.
Luffa, crosses, 232.
Lupines, heredity in, 106.
Lychnis Cœli-rosa, dwarfs, 144.
Lychnis, crosses, 240, 241.
Lycium, crosses, 218, 226.
Lycopods, crossing, 277.

Maize, crosses, 56.
Malle, Dureau de la, 175.
Mamillaria, sports, 194.
Maple, Wier's, 109.
Meadow, plants in, 23.
Medicago, crosses, 220, 233, 240.
Melandrium, crosses, 220, 222, 223, 225, 231, 233, 240, 244, 245.
Mendel, 239.
Mentha, bud-variety, 194.
Mentha, crosses, 229, 241.
Mersereau, 131.
Mimulus, crosses, 222, 251.
Mirabilis, crosses, 222, 226, 227, 228, 234, 241, 250, 251.
Mirabilis pollinations, 85.
Missing links, 41.
Mixing in the hill, 118, 201.
Molinia, bud-variety, 194.
Monœcious plants, 259.
Monotypic genera, 97.
Moore, Jacob, 110.
Morning-glory, 54.
Morong, Dr. Thomas, 60.

INDEX. 291

Morren, 149.
Mourrière, M., 175.
Mulberry, Teas', 109.
Multiple hybrids, 246, 247.
Munson, Professor, 58.
Munson, T. V., 79, 111.
Musa, bud-variety, 194.
Muskmelon pollination, 85.
Myrtle, bud-variety, 195.

Nanz & Neuner, 170.
Narcissus, crosses, 220, 225, 236.
Natal variations, 15.
Natural selection, 32, 51.
Naudin, 216, 229, 248.
Nectarine, origin of, 118, 173.
Nepenthes, crosses, 220.
Nicotiana, crosses, 72, 217, 219, 222, 224, 225, 226, 227, 229, 233, 234, 237, 238, 239, 241, 243, 244, 245, 246, 250.
Nicotiana pollinations, 85, 86.
Nuphar, crosses, 226.
Nymphaea, crosses, 218, 225, 227, 231, 234, 250.

Odoriferous varieties, 147.
Œnothera, crosses, 219, 239.
Œnothera Drummondii, dwarfs, 144.
Oger, Pierre, 166.
Olea ilicifolia, 195.
Opuntia, bud-variety, 195.
Orange, bud-variety, 195.
Orchideæ, crosses, 229, 233, 235.
Orchids, hybrids, 79.
Orontium, sport, 195.
Osmanthus, sport, 195.
Ovary, 255, 263.

Palmer, Asa, 139.
Pansy, 146.
Papaver, crosses, 218, 224, 226, 229, 231, 237.
Papaver, forms of, 151.
Paré, M., 160.
Parents, influence of, 81, 217.
Passiflora, crosses, 220, 226, 229, 235, 250.
Peach, bud-variation in, 118, 173, 196.
Peach, hybrids, 47.
Peaches, races of, 91.

Pear, bud-varieties, 174, 197.
Pears, hybrid, 66, 79, 111.
Pears, variation in, 99.
Peas, viney, 16.
Pelargonium, crosses, 218, 220, 229, 230, 233, 234, 237, 245, 246, 247.
Pelargonium, sports in, 198.
Peloric varieties, 152.
Pentstemon, crosses, 241.
Pepino pollinations, 86.
Pepino, variation in, 95.
Pepper, red, pollination, 85.
Peppers, variation in, 96.
Persica, 196.
Petal, 253.
Petunia, crosses, 218, 240, 241, 251.
Petunia pollinations, 85, 86.
Phalaris, sports, 198.
Phaseolus, crosses, 223, 238, 241.
Phlox, bud-varieties, 199.
Phragmites, bud-varieties, 199.
Physalis, 60.
Physalis, variation in, 96.
Picea, bud-variety, 199.
Pink, 156, 160.
Pinus, bud-varieties, 199.
Pinus, crosses, 226.
Pistil, 255.
Pisum, crosses, 223, 238.
Pittosporum, sport, 200.
Plant-breeding, 91.
Pliny, 131.
Plum, hybrids, 47, 112.
Plum, sports of, 172.
Plums, Japanese, 27.
Podocarpus, 155, 183.
Pollen, 254, 264.
Pollinating kit, 277, 278.
Pollination, 252.
Pollination, uncertainties of, 83.
Polymorphous varieties, 153.
Polytypic genera, 97.
Populus, bud-variety, 200.
Populus, crosses, 222.
Position, advantage of, 22.
Post-natal variations, 15.
Potamogeton, crosses, 227.
Potato, 37, 117.
Potato and tomato, 95.
Potato, bud-varieties, 201, 209.

Potato, seedlessness, 99.
Precocious varieties, 146.
Primula, crosses, 239, 240, 241.
Progeny of crosses, 237.
Proliferous varieties, 150.
Propagation, asexual, 7.
Pruning, 23.
Prunus, bud-variety, 205.
Prunus, crosses, 229, 239.
Pumpkin, crossing, 46, 58, 74, 82.
Pyrus, crosses, 229, 239.

Quercus, crosses, 226, 229, 239.
Quince, pollinated, 276.

Races in fruits, 90.
Radish pollinations, 85.
Raphanus Raphanistrum, 116, 231.
Raphanus sativus, 231.
Raspberry, flowering, 260.
Raspberry, hybrids, 79, 111.
Representative species, 66.
Retinosporas, 156.
Rheum, bud-variety, 206.
Rhododendron, crosses, 145, 218, 222, 225, 226, 229, 230, 239, 245, 246, 247.
Ribes, bud-varieties, 206.
Ribes, crosses, 230, 233.
Robinia, bud-varieties, 206.
Rogue, 89, 127.
Rosa, 161.
Rose, bud-varieties in, 118, 161, 207.
Roses, crosses, 233, 247.
Rubus, crosses, 227, 230, 232, 234.
Rubus odoratus, 260.
Running out of varieties, 36, 125.
Russia, fruits from, 27, 90, 133.
Rye, hybrids, 79.

Salix, bud-variety, 208.
Salix, crosses, 219, 225, 226, 227, 229, 231, 234, 239, 244, 245, 246, 247.
Salter, 119.
Salvia, crosses, 223.
Sambucus, sports, 208.
Satyrium hircinum, 148.
Scabiosa atropurpurea, dwarfs, 145.
Scalpel for pollinating, 270.
Schizanthus retusus, dwarfs, 145.
Scissors for pollinating, 270.

Secondary crosses, 238.
Seed, change of, 28, 59.
Seeds, colors of, 104.
Seeds, early, 147.
Seeds, immature, 103, 147.
Seeds, large and small, 101.
Selection and progress, 120, 122, 127
Selection, natural, 32, 51.
Self-fertilization, effects of, 54.
Senecio cruentus, dwarfs, 144.
Sepal, 253.
Seven-eighths hybrids, 243.
Sex and variation, 11, 43.
Silene, crosses, 234.
Sinningia, crosses, 231.
Solanum, bud-varieties, 209.
Solanum, variations in, 95.
Spencer, 61.
Spiraea, bud-varieties, 209.
Sports, 22, 28, 37, 153.
Sprengel, 54.
Squash, crosses, 58, 74, 82.
Squash flowers, 261.
Squash, Hubbard, 46.
Stamens, 254.
Stigma, 255.
Strawberry, Wilson, 125.
Struggle for life, 20, 29, 39.
Sturtevant, 103.
Style, 255.
Sugar-cane, varieties, 175.
Survival of the fittest, 32, 39.
Swamping effects of inter-crossing, 46.
Sweet, 247.
Symphoricarpus, sport, 209.
Symphytum, bud-varieties, 209.
Synchronistic variations, 117.

Tagetes, dwarfs, 145.
Teas, 109.
Teleology of hybrids, 236.
Thinning, 23.
Three-fourths hybrids, 243.
Thuyopsis, sport, 209.
Tillage and food supply, 17, 22.
Timbal-Lagrave, 217.
Toad-flax, 152.
Tobacco flowers, 266.
Tobacco pollinations, 86.
Tomato and potato, 95.

Tomato, crosses, 58.
Tomato, Ignotum, 123.
Tomato, pollinated, 276.
Tomato pollinations, 85.
Tomato, Trophy, 37.
Tomato, variation in, 98.
Tomatoes, breeding, 103.
Tragopogon, crosses, 238.
Triple hybrids, 244.
Tropaeolum, crosses, 222, 226.

Ulmus, bud-variety, 209.
Ulmus, crosses, 226.

Variability, variation in, 25.
Variation and environment, 12.
Variation caused by sex, 11, 43.
Variation, fortuitous, 9.
Variation, philosophy of, 1.
Variations, choice of, 31.
Variations, fixation of, 31.
Variations, natal and post-natal, 15.
Variations, origin of, 8, 41.   [157.
Variegation, perpetuating, 120, 149,
Varieties, running out, 36, 125.
Variety, what is a, 35.
Verbascum, crosses, 219, 221, 222, 223, 224, 226, 229, 235, 239, 250.

Verdier, Victor, 167.
Verlot, 121, 143.
Veronica, crosses, 233, 239.
Viburnum, sports, 209.
Vilmorin, 152.
Vilmorin, Henri L. de, 100, 105, 142.
Vilmorin, Louis Levêque de, 106.
Vine, bud-varieties, 174, 210.
Viola, bud-variety, 210.
Viola, crosses, 229, 231.
Vitis, crosses, 229, 239, 245, 246.

Walker, Ernest, 120, 169.
Wallace, 47, 60, 67.
Watermelon pollination, 85.
Weismann, 13, 14.
Wheat, hybrids, 79.
Wichura, 216, 246.
Wier, D. B., 109.
Wigandia, sport, 215.
Willdenow, 152.

Yucca, variation, 176.

Zinnia, crosses, 241.
Zinnia, flowers, 268.

NEW EDITION.

The Horticulturist's Rule-Book.

A COMPENDIUM OF USEFUL INFORMATION FOR FRUIT-GROWERS, TRUCK-GARDENERS, FLORISTS, AND OTHERS.

By L. H. BAILEY,
PROFESSOR OF HORTICULTURE IN THE CORNELL UNIVERSITY.

Third Edition, Thoroughly Revised and Recast, with Many Additions.

12mo. 302 pages. Limp Cloth. 75 cents.

This volume is the only attempt ever made in this country to codify and condense all the scattered rules, practices, recipes, figures, and histories relating to horticultural practice, in its broadest sense. It is much condensed, so that its three hundred pages comprise many thousand facts, the greater part of which the busy man would never possess if he were obliged to search them out in the voluminous literature of recent years. All the approved methods of fighting insects and plant diseases used and discovered by all the experiment stations are set forth in shape for instant reference. This feature alone is worth the making of the book.

Amongst the additions to the volume, in the present edition, are the following: A chapter upon "Greenhouse and Window-garden Work and Estimates," comprising full estimates and tables of heating glass-houses, lists of plants for forcing, for cut flowers, for window-gardens, aquaria, and the like, with temperatures at which many plants are grown, directions for making potting-earth and of caring for plants, etc.; a chapter on "Literature," giving classified and priced lists of the leading current books and periodicals on American horticulture, and directories of officers of whom the bulletins of the various experiment stations may be obtained; lists of self-fertile and self-sterile fruits; a full account of the methods of predicting frosts and of averting their injuries; a discussion of the aims and methods of phenology, or the record of climate in the blooming and leafing of trees; the rules of nomenclature adopted by botanists and by various horticultural societies; score-cards and scales of points for judging various fruits, vegetables, and flowers; a full statement of the metric system, and tables of foreign money.

THE MACMILLAN COMPANY,
66 FIFTH AVENUE, NEW YORK.

The Rural Science Series.

NOW READY.

The Soil. By FRANKLIN H. KING, Professor of Agricultural Physics, University of Wisconsin. 16mo. Cloth. 75 cents.

IN PRESS.

The Spraying of Plants. By ERNEST G. LODEMAN, Cornell University.

IN PREPARATION.

The Apple in North America. By L. H. BAILEY, Editor of the Series.

The Fertility of the Land. By I. P. ROBERTS, of Cornell University.

Milk and its Products. By H. H. WING.

Under the editorship of Professor L. H. Bailey of Cornell University, Macmillan & Co. purpose issuing a series of books upon agricultural subjects to be known as the **Rural Science Series.** Professor F. H. King, of the University of Wisconsin, has written upon **The Soil,** treating the subject from the new attitude which considers it as a scene of life rather than as a mere mechanical or chemical mixture. The physics of the soil are fully considered and the physical effects of fertilizers, drainage, and cultivation are discussed, as well as the adaptation of different types of soils to various crops. Professor I. P. Roberts, of Cornell University, will write upon **The Fertility of the Land.** This volume, while entirely independent of that of Professor King, will carry the subject directly into the practice of the field, giving a full discussion of the philosophy of plowing, cultivating, and the like, and an account of the best methods of maintaining and increasing the productivity of the land. The editor will contribute a monograph upon the cultivation of **The Apple in North America,** with a discussion of its evolution and the difficulties which now confront the apple-grower. **The Spraying of Plants** is treated by E. G. Lodeman of Cornell, in a comprehensive account of the origin and philosophy of the modern means of controlling insect and fungous troubles, and the application of these methods to the leading crops.

Some of the other volumes to be arranged for are:

Forestry.	Grape Culture.	Planting Manual.	Landscape Gardening.
Small Fruits.	Plant Life.	Rural Economics.	Etc., etc.

THE MACMILLAN COMPANY,
66 FIFTH AVENUE, NEW YORK.

WORKS BY L. H. BAILEY.

PROFESSOR OF HORTICULTURE IN CORNELL UNIVERSITY.

Talks Afield: About Plants and the Science of Plants. pp. 173. Illustrated.

Field Notes on Apple Culture. pp. 90. Illustrated.

The Horticulturist's Rule-Book: A Compendium of Useful Information for Fruit-Growers, Truck-Gardeners, Florists, and Others. Fourth edition. pp. 312.

The Nursery-Book: A Complete Guide to the Multiplication and Pollination of Plants. pp. 304. Illustrated.

American Grape Training. pp. 95. Illustrated.

Annals of Horticulture in North America for the Year 1889: A Witness of Passing Events and a Record of Progress. pp. 249. Illustrated.

Annals of Horticulture for 1890. pp. 312. Illustrated.

Annals of Horticulture for 1891. pp. 415. Illustrated.

Annals of Horticulture for 1892. pp. 387. Illustrated.

Annals of Horticulture for 1893: Comprising an Account of the Horticulture of the Columbian Exposition. pp. 179. Illustrated.

Gray's Field, Forest, and Garden Botany: A Simple Introduction to the Common Plants of the United States East of the 100th Meridian, Both Wild and Cultivated. Revised and extended by L. H. BAILEY, Editor of *The Rural Science Series* of agricultural and horticultural books.

Plant-Breeding: Being Five Lectures upon the Amelioration of Domestic Plants. pp. 293. Illustrated.

THE MACMILLAN COMPANY,
66 FIFTH AVENUE, NEW YORK.

www.ingramcontent.com/pod-product-compliance
Lightning Source LLC
Chambersburg PA
CBHW021955220426
43663CB00007B/827